Bilingual
THE CASTLES and CASTLE TOWNS of JAPAN

HIRAI-Kiyosi　　　Translated into English by Watanabe Hiroshi

日本の城と城下町
平井　聖

Bilingual THE CASTLES and CASTLE TOWNS of JAPAN by HIRAI-Kiyosi
Taiyaku NIHON no SIRO to ZYŌKAMATI
Copyright ©2017 Ichigayashuppansha
All rights reserved

Ichigaya Publishing Co.Ltd
市ヶ谷出版社

Preface: Castles and Castle Towns of the Edo Period

The word 'castle' conjures up an image of a white donjon seen against an azure sky. To its left and right are corner towers. The ensemble rises from a stone wall, and below that wall is a moat filled with water.

However, castles were originally the palaces of feudal lords. The fortification of such palaces led to the development of castles. The houses of samurai retainers, merchants who provided the necessities of life, and craftsmen who made weapons and tools for everyday life surrounded the lord's palace. In this way castle towns came into being.

A European castle surrounded by stone ramparts was also the residence of the lord of the castle. The houses of retainers, merchants and craftsmen were built around the residence, forming a town. Ramparts were built around those buildings as well to protect the warriors, merchants and craftsmen.

It is often said that no town in Japan was enclosed by a rampart, but that is not true. In Himezi, there are well preserved remains of earthwork—its lower parts protected by stone walls—that was intended to protect the castle and the middle enclosure where samurai of higher rank lived. The moat that once existed outside that earthwork has been filled in and turned into roads, but in the Edo period, it was a water-filled moat so wide that the area it once covered now accommodates not only a vehicular road but a sidewalk on both sides.

In Kanazawa, the castle town was surrounded by two layers of what was called a *sōgamae* (defensive perimeter), each layer consisting of earthwork and a water-filled moat. In Kanazawa, there were also rivers outside the outer defensive perimeter: Saigawa to the south and Asanogawa to the north. Beyond those rivers lay temple districts. Beyond the rivers, even as late as the end of the seventeenth century, nothing existed besides temples except *matiya* (townhouses) standing along highways.

On the *Gokaidō bunken nobe ezu* (Extended Survey Drawings of the Five Highways), drawn in the Edo period, only farming villages are shown until the next post station, once one is beyond the outskirts of a town.

The capitals of ancient Japan such as Heizyōkyō and Heiankyō were influenced by cities in continental China. Those cities had high fortified walls built of stone. The fortified wall around Beijing has been demolished, but Xi'an is still completely enclosed by a fortified wall even today. Modeled on cities on the continent, both Heizyōkyō and Heiankyō had grid-patterned streets and a palace located in the center to the north. However, neither had a fortified wall. In the sixteenth century, Toyotomi Hideyosi enclosed Kyoto, which was built on what had been Heiankyō, in an earthen embankment called the Odoi.

In Japanese castle towns of the feudal period, crossroads were avoided as much as possible in anticipation of invasion by an enemy. To prevent clear views, T-type intersections and staggered crossings were used instead. This too is a special characteristic of Japanese castle towns.

The castles and castle towns of Japan demonstrate great creativity and are unique to this country. Visitors are urged not only to look at donjons but to walk about and examine the organization of castle towns and the appearance of surviving *matiya*.

July 2017   HIRAI-Kiyosi

まえがき —— 江戸時代の城と城下町—

　城というと、青空に映える、白亜の天守を思い浮かべる。天守の左右には隅櫓があり、それらを支える石垣があり、石垣の下には水堀がある。

　しかし、城は本来領主の屋形であった。その領主の屋形を武装して、城ができた。さらに、城主の屋形を、家来である武士の家、生活を支えた商人の家、武器や生活用具を作る職人の住まいが囲んで、城下町ができた。

　ヨーロッパの石の城壁で囲まれた城でも、城は領主の住まいであった。その周りに家来の家、商人の家、職人の家が集まって、街が出来た。武士、商人や職人の街を守るために、さらにその外側に城壁ができた。

　日本では、街を囲む城壁がないという。そんなことはない。姫路には、城と上級武士の住む中郭を守るための、裾を石垣で固めた土塁がよく残っている。その前にあった堀は、埋められて道路になっているが、江戸時代には、車道だけでなく、両側の歩道部分までも含んだ、幅の広い水堀があった。

　金沢では、総構と呼ばれた土塁と水堀が、二重に城下町を囲んでいた。その外側の水堀には、今でも水がとうとうと流れている。金沢では、外惣構のさらに外側に、川があった。南は犀川、北は浅野川である。川の外側には、寺町があった。川の外は、17世紀の終わりころでも、寺院のほかには、街道に面して町屋が並ぶだけであった。

　江戸時代に描かれた『五街道分間延絵図』を見ても、町境を越えると次の宿場まで、間にあるのは農村だけである。

　古代の日本の町、例えば平城京や平安京は、中国大陸の都市の影響を受けている。中国大陸の都市には、石で築かれた高い城壁があった。北京の外側の城壁は取り払われたが、西安は、今でも完全に城壁で囲まれている。平城京や平安京では、大陸の都市に倣って、碁盤目状に街を造り、中央北部に宮殿を置いたが、城壁は築かなかった。豊臣秀吉は、平安京を基にした京の都を、16世紀になって御土居で囲んだ。

　近世の日本の城下町では、敵が町に侵入した時を考えて、なるべく十字路を造らず、見通せないように、道をT字形に交差させたり、あるいはクランク状に曲げたりしている。これも日本の城下町の特徴であろう。

　日本の城と城下町には、日本独特の創意がある。ただ天守を見るだけでなく、街を歩き、城下町の構成や、残っている町屋の姿にも目を向けてほしい。

2017年7月

平井　聖

Ichigaya Publishing's Bilingual Architecture Series

As international contacts increase year by year, it becomes ever more important to deepen our understanding of different cultures. In this endeavor, the greatest obstacle in our way is inevitably the language barrier. The fact that the Japanese language is hardly used outside of Japan has proved the most serious stumbling block for Japanese involved in international enterprises. English, on the other hand, though it cannot claim to be an entirely rational language, does have notable virtues of simplicity, flexibility, and power to coin words, as well as the enormous advantage of the phonetic roman alphabet, which can be used without the introduction of complex additional symbols. Now the dominant language of the electronic media, English has become an international language.

Several experimental projects led us to the conclusion that the production of Japanese-English bilingual texts by a Japanese-based publisher would not only meet international demand, but also be of service to Japanese readers. They can begin to familiarize themselves with the English language, and can even use the English text to cross-check ambiguities in the Japanese. It also goes without saying that the juxtaposition of the Japanese text beside the English one can only help the spread of Japanese abroad.

With all these factors in mind, Ichigaya publishing is planning to produce a series of bilingual text books on architecture. We sincerely hope that this series will be of service to Japanese students of architecture wishing to study in English; to foreign students of architecture who need a guide to Japanese architectural terminology, and to foreign students of the Japanese language, as well as all those interested in Japan's architectural traditions, which constitute such an important element in Japanese culture.

Ichigaya Publishing, July 2017

「日本建築バイリンガルテキスト」刊行について

　世界がひとつになる時代を迎えて，異質の文化を，相互に，より深く理解することがますます重要になってきた。その最大の障害となっているのが，いわゆる「言葉の壁」である。特に日本語は，日本以外の国ではほとんど用いられることがなく，日本人の国際的活動にあたっての最大のハンディキャップとなっている。

　これに対し，英語は必ずしも合理的な言語とはいえないが，簡潔性，柔軟性，造語力の点できわめてすぐれており，さらにアルファベットに煩雑な付加記号を加える必要がいっさいないという表記法上の大きな長所があって，電子機器にも最もよく適合し，実質上，すでに国際語としての地位を確立している。

　さまざまな試みののち，日本語による出版物は，日英二か国語のバイリンガルの本とすることが，最もよく国際的に通用するばかりでなく，日本人読者にとっても有益であることがわかってきた。単に英語を身近なものにする端緒となるばかりでなく，日本語ではしばしば意味があいまいになる部分を，英語で確かめることができるからである。

　また，日本語の国際的普及の方法としても，日本語に常に英語を併置することが最も有効であることはいうまでもない。

　このような考えから，市ヶ谷出版社は，まず建築学という分野で，バイリンガルのテキストを逐次刊行するという計画を立てた。英語を通じて建築学を学びたい日本人ばかりでなく，日本語を通じて日本文化の重要な部分を構成する日本の歴史的建築，伝統的建築および現代建築を知りたい外国人が、このバイリンガルテキストを十分に活用して下さることを心から願っている。

2017 年 7 月　　　　　　　　　　　　　　　　　　　　　　　　　　　　　　市ヶ谷出版社

Contents

Castles and Castle Towns of the Edo Period ·· 1

01 The Inner Enclosures of Himezi Castle According to the Nakane Drawing ············· 2
02 The Present Condition of Himezi Castle ·· 4
03 The Organization of the Inner Enclosures··· 6
04 The Main Enclosure (Including Donjons) ·· 8
05 The Caltrop Gate and the Western Enclosure ···10
06 The Residence in the Tertiary Enclosure (The Western Estate) ·····························12
07 The Opposite Estate in the Tertiary Enclosure ···14
08 The Musasino Residence and Sakuziba ··16
09 The Organization of the Outer Enclosure (Castle Town) 1. ·····································18
10 The Organization of the Outer Enclosure (Castle Town) 2. ·····································20
11 Earthworks and Moats around Castles ··22
12 The Defensive Perimeter of Kanazawa Castle ···24
13 The Locations of Castles 1. Hill-on-the-Plain Castles ···26
14 The Locations of Castles 2. Mountain Castles ···28
15 The Locations of Castles 3. The Remains of Asakura Castle Town in Itizyōdani ······30
16 The Locations of Castles 4. Plain Castles ··32
17 The Organization of Castle Towns 1. ··34
18 The Organization of Castle Towns 2. ··36
19 The Organization of Castle Towns 3. ··38
20 Enclosing a Castle Town 1. ··40
21 Enclosing a Castle Town 2. ··42
22 Enclosing a Castle Town 3. ··44
23 Laying Stone Walls 1. ···46
24 Laying Stone Walls 2. ···48
25 Laying Stone Walls 3. ···50
26 The Facilities of a Castle Town 1. Guard Stations ···52
27 The Facilities of a Castle Town 2. Fire Watchtowers ···54
28 The Facilities of a Castle Town 3. Water Supply 1.···56
29 The Facilities of a Castle Town 4. Water Supply 2.···58
30 The Facilities of a Castle Town 5. Theaters ···60
31 The Facilities of a Castle Town 6. Bath Houses ···62
32 The Development of the Feudal Castle 1.···64
33 The Development of the Feudal Castle 2.···66
34 Constructing a Castle 1. Location ··68
35 Constructing a Castle 2. Site Plan ···70

目　次

江戸時代の城と城下町……………………………………………………… 1
01　中根図の姫路城内郭………………………………………………… 2
02　姫路城の現状………………………………………………………… 4
03　内郭内の構成………………………………………………………… 6
04　本丸（天守郭を含む）……………………………………………… 8
05　菱の門、西の丸…………………………………………………… 10
06　三の丸の御居城（西屋敷）……………………………………… 12
07　三の丸の向屋敷…………………………………………………… 14
08　武蔵野御殿・作事場……………………………………………… 16
09　外郭（城下町）の構成－1……………………………………… 18
10　外郭（城下町）の構成－2……………………………………… 20
11　城を囲む土塁と堀………………………………………………… 22
12　金沢城の総構……………………………………………………… 24
13　城の立地－1　平山城…………………………………………… 26
14　城の立地－2　山城……………………………………………… 28
15　城の立地－3　一乗谷朝倉氏遺跡……………………………… 30
16　城の立地－4　平城……………………………………………… 32
17　城下町の構成－1………………………………………………… 34
18　城下町の構成－2………………………………………………… 36
19　城下町の構成－3………………………………………………… 38
20　城下町を囲む－1………………………………………………… 40
21　城下町を囲む－2………………………………………………… 42
22　城下町を囲む－3………………………………………………… 44
23　石垣を積む－1…………………………………………………… 46
24　石垣を積む－2…………………………………………………… 48
25　石垣を積む－3…………………………………………………… 50
26　城下町の施設－1　番所………………………………………… 52
27　城下町の施設－2　火の見……………………………………… 54
28　城下町の施設－3　水道－1…………………………………… 56
29　城下町の施設－4　水道－2…………………………………… 58
30　城下町の施設－5　芝居小屋…………………………………… 60
31　城下町の施設－6　湯屋　風呂屋……………………………… 62
32　近世の城が出来るまで－1……………………………………… 64
33　近世の城が出来るまで－2……………………………………… 66
34　城の構成－1　地選・地取り…………………………………… 68
35　城の構成－2　縄張り…………………………………………… 70

36	Constructing a Castle 3. Constructing a Donjon 1.	72
37	Constructing a Castle 4. Constructing a Donjon 2.	74
38	Constructing a Castle 5. Constructing the Donjons of Himezi Castle	76
39	The Structure and Design of Donjons and Towers 1.	78
40	The Structure and Design of Donjons and Towers 2.	80
41	The Structure and Design of Donjons and Towers 3.	82
42	The Structure and Design of Donjons and Towers 4.	84
43	The Structure and Design of Donjons and Towers 5. *Yazama, Teppōzama, Isiotosi*	86
44	The Facilities of a Castle 1.	88
45	The Facilities of a Castle 2.	90
46	Building Construction Work 1. *Husin* and *Sakuzi*	92
47	Building Construction Work 2. Architectural Drawings 1.	94
48	Building Construction Work 3. Architectural Drawings 2.	96
49	Building Construction Work 4. Construction	98
50	Building Construction Work 5. Walls	100
51	Building Construction Work 6. Roofing	102
52	Building Construction Work 7. Ridge, *Ōmune, Kudarimune, Sumimune, Onigawara, Syati*	104
53	Building Construction Work 8. Ceremonies of Carpenters	106
54	Building Construction Work 9. Carpenter's Tools	108
55	Residence in the Castle and Residences of Retainers outside the Castle -1 (*Syoin-zukuri*)	110
56	Residence in the Castle and Residences of Retainers outside the Castle -2 (Before the Development of the *Syoin* Style)	112
57	Residence in the Castle and Residences of Retainers outside the Castle 3. Residences of Retainers outside the Castle	114
58	Residence in the Castle and Residences of Retainers outside the Castle 4. Daimyō Estates Dedicated to Pastimes and Buildings for Relaxation	116

Castles in Various Areas of Japan (1 ~ 74) ··· 118

Illustration Credits ··· 151

Index and Glossary ··· 153

36	城の構成－3　天守の構成－1	72
37	城の構成－4　天守の構成－2	74
38	城の構成－5　姫路城の天守の構成	76
39	天守・櫓の構造と意匠－1	78
40	天守・櫓の構造と意匠－2	80
41	天守・櫓の構造と意匠－3	82
42	天守・櫓の構造と意匠－4	84
43	天守の外観構成と意匠－5　矢狭間　鉄砲狭間　石落し	86
44	城の施設－1　門－1	88
45	城の施設－2　門－2	90
46	建築工事－1　普請と作事	92
47	建築工事－2　建築図面－1	94
48	建築工事－3　建築図面－2	96
49	建築工事－4　軸組構法	98
50	建築工事－5　壁	100
51	建築工事－6　屋根を葺く	102
52	建築工事－7　棟（大棟・下り棟・隅棟）、鬼瓦・鯱	104
53	建築工事－8　大工の儀式	106
54	建築工事－9　大工道具	108
55	城内の御殿・城下の藩士の屋敷（書院造）－1	110
56	城内の御殿・城下の藩士の屋敷（書院造が出来るまで）－2	112
57	城内の御殿・城下の藩士の屋敷－3　城下の家臣たちの住まい	114
58	城内の御殿・城下の藩士の屋敷－4　大名の遊びの屋敷、ゆとりの建物	116

日本各地の城（1～74） …………………………………………………………… 118

掲載図版所蔵先 …………………………………………………………………… 151

索引　英語 ………………………………………………………………………… 153
　　　専門用語 …………………………………………………………………… 157
　　　城 ………………………………………………………………………… 161
　　　人名 ……………………………………………………………………… 163

Terms indicating historical periods used in this book.

Medieval period：Kamakura period and Muromati period 1185~1573
Period of Warring States：Kamakura period and Muromati period 1467~1573
Feudal：Azuti-Momoyama period and Edo period 1568~1868
Edo Period：1603~1868

本書の中で使っている時代を示す用語

中　　世　鎌倉時代および室町時代　文治元年（1185）～天正元年（1573）
戦国時代　応仁元年（1467）～天正元年（1573）
近　　世　安土桃山時代および江戸時代　永禄11年（1568）～慶応4年（1868）
江戸時代　慶長8年（1603）～慶応4年（1868）

The Kunrei-shiki system established by the Japanese Ministry of Education is used in this book to romanize Japanese terms.

本書で使用している日本語のローマ字表記は、文部省が定めた訓令式です。

「ローマ字のつづり方」（昭和29年12月9日　内閣告示第1号）の第1表

第1表　〔（　）は重出を示す。〕

a	i	u	e	o			
ka	ki	ku	ke	ko	kya	kyu	kyo
sa	si	su	se	so	sya	syu	syo
ta	ti	tu	te	to	tya	tyu	tyo
na	ni	nu	ne	no	nya	nyu	nyo
ha	hi	hu	he	ho	hya	hyu	hyo
ma	mi	mu	me	mo	mya	myu	myo
ya	(i)	yu	(e)	yo			
ra	ri	ru	re	ro	rya	ryu	ryo
wa	(i)	(u)	(e)	(o)			
ga	gi	gu	ge	go	gya	gyu	gyo
za	zi	zu	ze	zo	zya	zyu	zyo
da	(zi)	(zu)	de	do	(zya)	(zyu)	(zyo)
ba	bi	bu	be	bo	bya	byu	byo
pa	pi	pu	pe	po	pya	pyu	pyo

THE CASTLES and CASTLE TOWNS of the Edo Period

江戸時代の城と城下町

Drawing of Himezi Castle："Bansyū Himezi-zyō no zu."（Tadayuki Nakane）
姫路城図『播州姫路城図』（中根忠之蔵）

01 The Inner Enclosures of Himezi Castle According to the Nakane Drawing

This drawing of the inner enclosures of Himezi Castle in their entirety has been handed down in the Nakane family whose members served as senior retainers of the Honda clan. The Hondas were twice lords of Himezi Castle during the Edo period. From its details, the drawing appears to show the castle as it was around 1700 during the second occupation.

The Honda clan took possession of Himezi Castle for the second time in 1682 and left it in 1704. If the shrine shown in the drawing is Osakabe Shrine, which was built in 1699, it follows that the drawing shows what the layout of the castle was like between 1699 and 1704.

01　中根図の姫路城内郭

　この姫路城内郭の全景を描いた絵図は、かつて姫路の藩主であった本多家に家老として仕えた中根家に伝えられています。本多家は、江戸時代に二度姫路城主を務めました。この図に描かれた姫路城は、描かれた内容から、二度目に姫路城主であった時代の姫路城の様子、1700年頃と考えられています。

　本多家が二度目に姫路城に入ったのは1682年、姫路を去ったのが1704年です。さらに、この図に描かれている神社が長壁神社とすれば、長壁神社が祀られたのが1699年ですから、1699年から1704年までの間の様子ということになります。

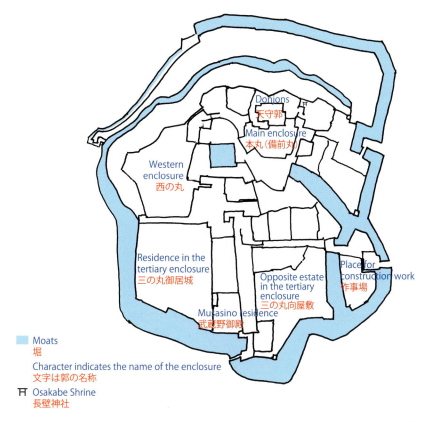

The present condition of the inner enclosures of Himezi Castle, prepared from a Geographical Survey Institute map.
姫路城内郭部の現状（「姫路市都市計画図」（姫路市作成））。図をもとに加工。青・赤文字は江戸時代の区分。

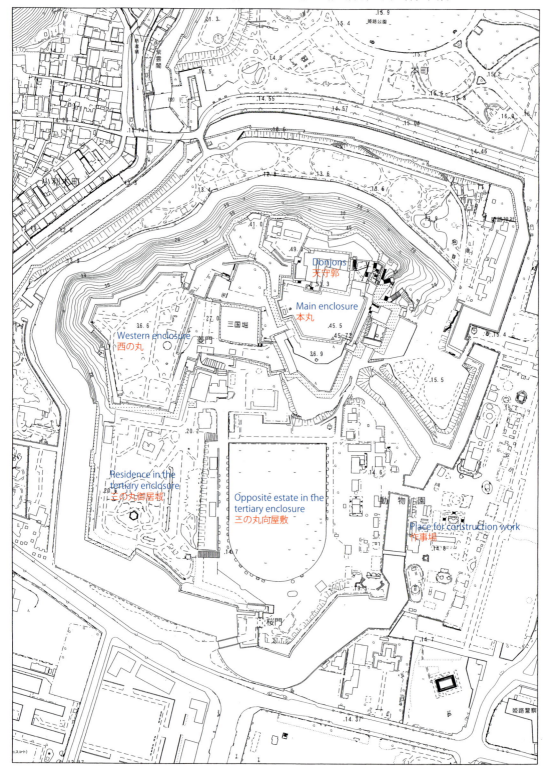

02 The Present Condition of Himezi Castle

This drawing, showing the inner enclosures (*utiguruwa*) of Himezi Castle as they are now, is based on a present-day map.

A comparison of the Nakane drawing and this drawing shows that the moats (*hori*) and stone walls (*isigaki*) both inside and outside the inner enclosures have remained virtually unchanged. The moat to the east of the enclosure that was referred to as a place for construction work (*sakuziba*) has been filled in, so that this area, now occupied by a zoo, is no longer cut off from the rest of the grounds.

At the time the Nakane drawing was made, many residential buildings stood in the tertiary enclosure (*sannomaru*), and some of the residential buildings survived even in the western enclosure (*nisinomaru*) and the main enclosure (*hommaru*). However, those buildings are no longer extant.

By comparison, the donjons (*tensyu*) that are the symbols of the castle and the two-storied towers (*nizyū-yagura*) and *tamon-yagura* (long, narrow buildings constructed along stone walls) that surround the main and western enclosures survive for the most part and make the inner enclosures of Himezi Castle an impressive sight even from a distance.

02 姫路城の現状

現在の地図をもとに、現在の**姫路城内郭部**を示しています。

中根図と現状図を比較すると、**内郭**（うちぐるわ）を取り巻く堀や石垣、そしてその内部の石垣や堀が、ほとんど変わっていないことがわかります。作事場と呼ばれた郭（くるわ）の東側の堀が埋められたので、作事場は地続きになっています。現在、このあたりは動物園です。

中根図の時代には、**三の丸**には多くの御殿が建っていましたし、**西の丸**や**本丸**にも一部の御殿が残っていました。しかし、これらの御殿は、現在全くありません。

それに対して、城のシンボルである**天守群**や、本丸・西の丸などを囲む**多聞櫓**や**二重櫓**などはよく残っていて、遠くから眺めると、姫路城内郭部の威容がよくわかります。

Himezi Castle,
姫路城

Three-dimensional representation of the residence and other structures, based on plans in "Bansyū Himezi-zyō no zu."
『播州姫路城図』中の御殿等をその平面図に基づいて立体化

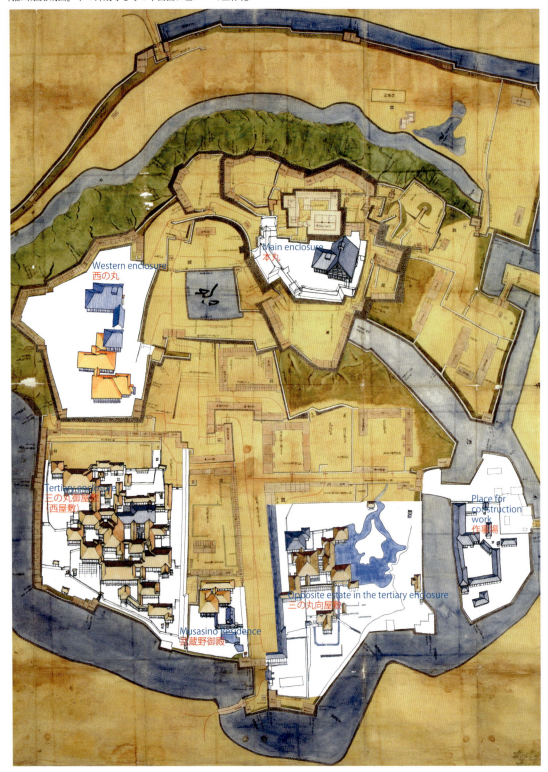

03   The Organization of the Inner Enclosures

The inner enclosures of Himezi Castle included the main enclosure (*hommaru*), secondary enclosure (*ninomaru*), tertiary enclosure (*sannomaru*) and western enclosure (*nisinomaru*). Different levels of the hill known as Himeyama were demarcated to form these enclosures, with the main enclosure containing the donjons (*tensyu*) situated at the highest point and the tertiary enclosure at the lowest.

Himezi was an example of a hill-on-the-plain castle (*hirayamaziro*), a type of castle in which donjons were constructed at the highest point; the area around them was made the main enclosure. The secondary enclosure was arranged at a lower level, and the tertiary enclosure below that. Of the inner enclosures of Himezi Castle, the tertiary enclosure was the largest in area, and the lord of the castle lived in a residence in that enclosure.

Other enclosures included the northwestern enclosure (*inuinokuruwa*) and western enclosure (*nisinomaru*) named for their respective orientation, the well enclosure (*idonokuruwa*) where the well was located, the garden enclosure (*yamazatoguruwa*) where a landscape with a mountain was recreated, and the place for construction work (*sakuziba*) where carpenters and plasterers toiled.

03　内郭内の構成

　姫路城の内部は、本丸をはじめ二の丸・三の丸・西の丸などに分かれています。

　これらの**郭**は姫山の高低を利用して区画され、一番高い所に天守を擁する本丸を置き、一番低い郭を三の丸としています。

　姫路城のような**平山城**では、最も高い所に天守群を建て、その周囲を本丸としています。低くなるに従って、二の丸・三の丸が配置されています。姫路城内郭の中では、三の丸が最も広く、城主は三の丸の御殿に住んでいました。

　本丸・二の丸・三の丸のほかに、方位によって名付けられた乾郭、西の丸、井戸のある井戸郭、山里の景観を造り出した山里郭、大工や左官などが詰めている作事場などがありました。

Conjectural restoration of the residence of the main enclosure (Bizen-maru) in "Bansyū Himezi-zyō no zu."
『播州姫路城図』の本丸（備前丸）部分の御殿の推定復元

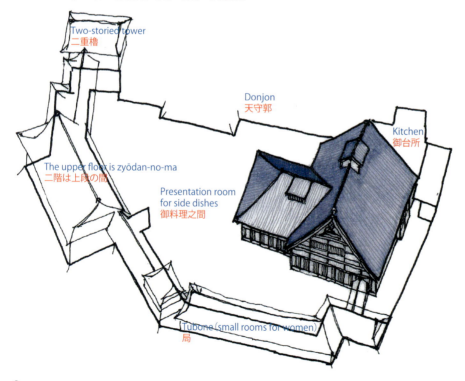

04   The Main Enclosure (Including Donjons)

Donjons   Buildings painted white shown on the north side in the Nakane drawing are the donjons. They consist of the main donjon (*daitensyu*) and three minor donjons (*kotensyu*).

Residence of the Main Enclosure   On the stone wall of the west side of the open space below the donjons are shown two connected rooms. The room labeled *zyōdan-no-ma* appears to have had a decorative alcove (*tokonoma*). On the south side stone wall are shown a string of small rooms called *tubone*.

However, in the open space of the main enclosure, there exist only the "preparation room for side dishes" (*oryōri-no-ma*) and the "kitchen" (*odaidokoro*). Residential quarters and a *syoin*-style room must have originally stood there as well.

The only entrance to the main enclosure is the gate drawn in front of the kitchen. The front entrance for the residence of the main compound may have been in the structure labeled "two-storied tower" (*nizyūyagura*) near the western minor donjon.

04   本丸（天守郭を含む）

　天守郭　　中根図には、北側に白く塗られた建物群があります。これが**天守郭**（てんしゅぐるわ）です。天守郭を構成しているのは**大天守**と三つの**小天守**です。中根図では、大天守は「二重目」とあり、石垣の上の階を描いています。現在はこの階を一階と呼び、その下の石垣の中の階を穴蔵と考えています。

　本丸の御殿　　天守群の下の広場をみると、西側の石垣上に、二室連なる上段の間があり、「上段間」と書き込まれた部屋には、床の間があったようです。南側の石垣上には女性が住んだ「局（つぼね）」の小さな部屋が並んでいます。

　しかし、本丸の広場には、「御料理之間」と「御台所」しかありません。最初は居間や書院などが建っていたのでしょう。

　本丸には、中根図で赤い線が引かれている台所の前の門しか、入口がありません。西の小天守に近い二重櫓に、本丸御殿への表の入口があったのかもしれません。

Conjectural restoration of the residence of the western enclosure in "Bansyū Himezi-zyō no zu."
『播州姫路城図』の西の丸部分の御殿の推定復元

05 The Caltrop Gate and the Western Enclosure

Caltrop Gate   The blue square labeled *ike* (pond) below and to the left of the main enclosure on the Nakane drawing is the Three-Province Moat (Sangokubori). Below and to the left of this moat is the Caltrop Gate (Hisi no Mon). This is a *yaguramon*, a type of two-storied gatehouse widely used in castles.

The Residence of the Western Enclosure   Passing through the Caltrop Gate and climbing the road on the left-hand side, one arrived at the western enclosure. Today, only corridor-like *tamon-yagura*, angle towers (*sumi-yagura*), walls and the Dowry Tower (Kesyō Yagura) rise above the stone walls, but structures such as an entrance (*genkan*), reception hall (*hiroma*), kitchen (*daidokoro*), and storehouse (*dozō*) are indicated in the Nakane drawing. Honda Tadamasa, who became lord of Himezi Castle in 1617, constructed the western enclosure on the occasion of the marriage of his son, Tadatoki, to Sen Hime, the daughter of the second Tokugawa shōgun, Tokugawa Hidetada. Much time has passed since then; no doubt the missing buildings were destroyed.

The corridors in the Nakane drawing do not connect to buildings at right angles. The entrance hall and other buildings are not parallel to each other. This suggests that the original building plans, made from separate colored pieces of paper that were then glued to the mount, came off in time and had to be reattached again. The Nakane drawing must be a copy of an imperfectly repaired original plan by someone not knowledgeable in architecture.

05 菱の門、西の丸

　菱の門　　中根図の本丸の左下、「池」と書かれた青い四角は、三国堀です。三国堀の左下が「菱ノ御門」で、城の門によく使われる櫓門です。

　西の丸の御殿　　菱の門を入って左側の道を登ると、西の丸です。今は周囲の石垣の上に、多聞櫓と隅櫓、塀そして化粧櫓しかありませんが、中根図では、玄関と広間、台所、土蔵等が描かれています。西の丸は、1617年に姫路城主として入った本多忠政が、嫡男忠刻の嫁に二代将軍徳川秀忠の娘の千姫を迎えるにあたって築きました。千姫が住んでいたころから時間がたっていますので、ほかのいくつかの建物は壊されたでのしょう。

　中根図では、建物と建物をつなぐ廊下が、直角につながっていません。玄関とほかの建物が、平行に並んでいません。このことは、元の図面が、台紙に別の色紙で作った建物平面を貼り付けて作られていた貼絵図（94頁参照）で、時代とともに貼った建物平面がはがれ、貼りなおしたことを物語っています。原図を、建築が専門でない人が書き写して、この図面が作られたという経過を示唆しています。

Conjectural restoration of the residence of the tertiary enclosure in "Bansyū Himezi-zyō no zu."
『播州姫路城図』の三の丸御居城部分の御殿の推定復元

06 The Residence in the Tertiary Enclosure (The Western Estate)

The residence of the lord of the castle was on high ground on the west side of the road leading south from the Caltrop Gate.

From south to north, the interconnected buildings of the residence included the entrance hall, Crane Room (Turu no Ma), Kurosyoin, New Syoin, food preparation room, living room, sleeping room and room for rest. In addition, there were a Nō stage, a large kitchen, and a bath.

In a drawing introduced by Mr. Masatugu Hasimoto, the entrance hall is labeled "Tiger Room" (Tora no Ma), and a boarded area (*sikidai*) is attached to it. In the Nakane drawing, a two-story rooms has been added to the side of the *sikidai*, and the room no longer serves as the entrance. There is also no room for rest in Mr. Hasimoto's drawing. The layout of the New Syoin is different; there is no *sukiya* (tea room). Mr. Hashimoto's drawing in all likelihood shows an earlier arrangement.

06 三の丸の御居城（西屋敷）

菱の門から南への道の西側の高台にあったのが、**城主の住居**です。

御殿は、南から北へ、玄関、鶴の間、小書院、新書院、その北の料理の間、居間と寝間、休息ノ間へと続きます。これらの御殿に、能舞台、大きな台所、御風呂屋などが加わります。

橋本政次氏が紹介された絵図では、玄関は「とらの間」です。「とらの間」には、入口の敷台が付属しています。中根図の「虎之御間」には、敷台の脇に二階建ての部分が増築されていて、入り口ではなくなっています。また、橋本氏の絵図には、休息ノ間がありません。新書院の中の間取りが違い数寄屋（茶室）がありません。橋本氏の絵図のほうが、古い時代の様子を示しているのでしょう。

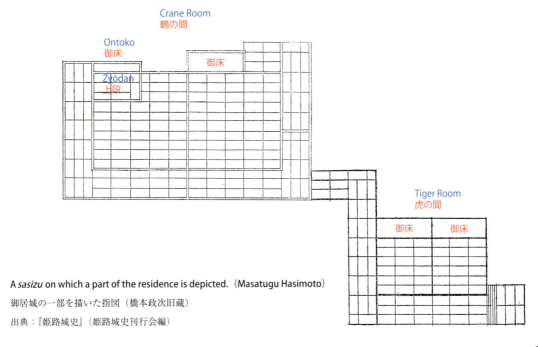

A *sasizu* on which a part of the residence is depicted. (Masatugu Hasimoto)

御居城の一部を描いた指図（橋本政次旧蔵）

出典：『姫路城史』（姫路城史刊行会編）

Conjectural restoration of the residence in the opposite estate in the tertiary enclosure of "Bansyū Himezi-zyō no zu"
『播州姫路城図』の三の丸向屋敷の部分の御殿の推定復元

07 The Opposite Estate in the Tertiary Enclosure

On the east side of the road heading south from the Caltrop Gate was the so-called "opposite estate" (*mukai yasiki*). The opposite estate had a garden with a hillock and a pond in the middle of which was an island. There were also a bath house surrounded by a watercourse, a number of *sukiya* (tea rooms) and, just inside a large entrance hall, a so-called "Umbrella Room" (Karakasa no Ma). These suggest that this was a place for relaxation and diversion. However, no record of this estate being used has been discovered.

The Umbrella Room was a unique feature of this residence. A large room measuring eight *ken* square (15.76 m square), it had only one post in the middle. This post was three *syaku* square (.909 m square) in cross section. Beams corresponding to the ribs of an umbrella may have radiated in all directions downward from the top of the post and been supported midway by diagonal struts rising from the post. As with the ribs of an umbrella, the structure would not have needed any supports on the perimeter. There was a long hearth in this room. One can only guess how this room was used.

07 三の丸の向屋敷

　菱の門から南への道の東側に、中島のある大きな池や築山のある、**向屋敷**（むかいやしき）があります。この向屋敷には水路で囲まれた風呂屋、幾つかの数寄屋（茶室）、大きな玄関を入ったところにある「唐笠間（からかさのま）」などがあって、くつろぎ、遊びの場であったことがわかります。しかし、この屋敷を使った時の記録が見つかっていません。

　向屋敷の中でも特殊なのは「唐笠間」です。8間四方もある大きな部屋で、柱は真ん中に1本あるだけです。その柱は、3尺角。構造を推理すると、傘の骨に当たる登り梁が周囲から頂点に向かって放射状にかかり、頂点をまとめ、登り梁の真ん中あたりを、中央の太い柱から斜め上に向かう材で支えていたのではないかと思います。傘の骨のように周囲には支える柱はなくてもいいのです。この部屋には、長い炉がありました。どのように使ったのでしょうか。

唐笠の間の構造（推定）
Construction of Karakasa no Ma

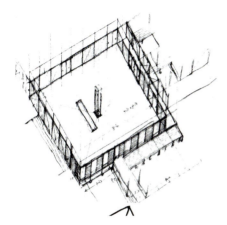
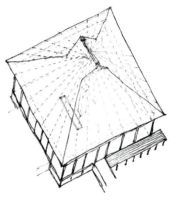

08 The Musasino Residence and Sakuziba

Musasino Residence   The Musasino Residence was on the left-hand side on the road from the Cherry Gate (Sakura no Mon) to the Caltrop Gate. It was surrounded by long, narrow buildings (*nagaya*). Three buildings are shown inside it in the drawing, but they had apparently already fallen into disuse by that time.

Sakuziba (Place for Construction Work)   This is an enclosure surrounded by a moat to the east of the tertiary enclosure. There are places designated as the master carpenter's drawing office, drawing room, carpenters' room, plasterers' room, timberyard storage space for boards, ropes, and straws, and stove for simmering seaweed to paste. Absent are places for other construction-related work such as the manufacture of nails and ornamental metalware and the application of paints and coatings such as lacquer. There are also no rooms for the masons who laid stone walls or gardeners.

Conjectural restoration of the Musasino Residence in "Bansyū Himezi-zyō no zu"
『播州姫路城図』の武蔵野御殿部分の御殿の推定復元

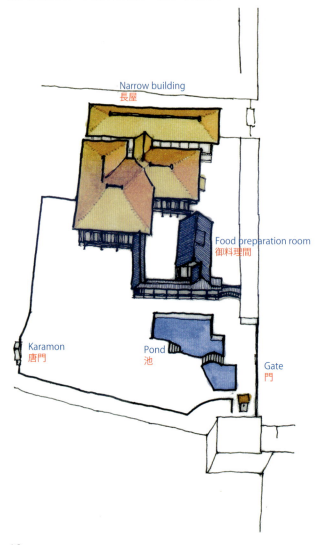

08 武蔵野御殿・作事場

　武蔵野御殿　桜門から菱の門へ向かう道へ回り込むと、左側に武蔵野御殿があります。廻りを長屋が囲み、中に 3 棟の建物が描かれていますが、描かれた当時、すでに使われなくなって、放置されていたのではないかと思います。

　作事場　三の丸の東に堀で囲まれた 1 郭があります。「絵図所」「絵図小屋」「大工小屋」「瓦小屋」「左官小屋」「材木小屋」「板小屋」「すさ小屋」「縄小屋」「藁小屋」「釜屋」があります。建築工事では、釘などを作る鍛冶屋、飾金具を作る飾屋、漆などの塗装をする塗師の部屋がありません。建築以外では、石垣を積む穴太、植木職人の部屋もありません。

Conjectural restoration of buildings in the sakuziba in "Bansyū Himezi-zyō no zu."
『播州姫路城図』の作事場部分の建物の推定復元

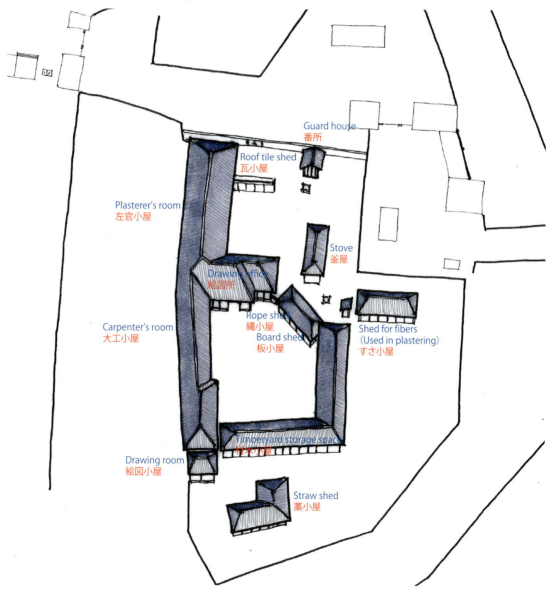

"Himezi osiro mawari samurai yasiki sin ezu" (New Drawing of Samurai Estates around Himezi Castle). (Himeji center for Research into Castles and Fortifications)

『姫路御城廻侍屋舗新絵図』(姫路市立城郭研究室蔵)

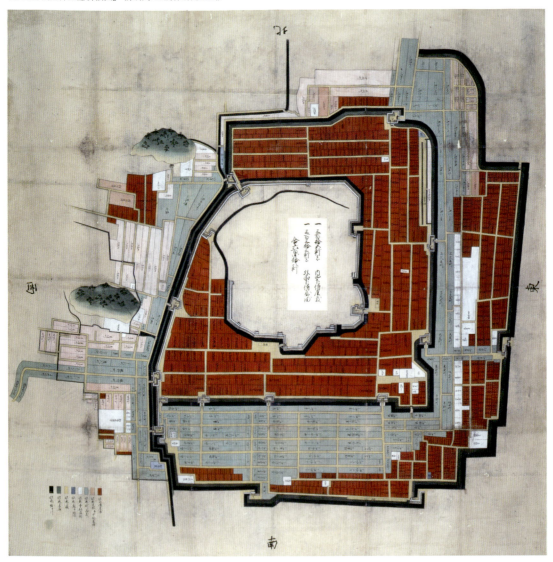

09 The Organization of the Outer Enclosure (Castle Town) 1.

A feudal castle is what is built inside a large outer defensive perimeter (*sotosōgamae*). It is often said that in Japanese castles walls did not enclose entire towns or cities as they often did in European castles and the walled cities of China. However, there were castle towns (*zyōka mati*) such as Himezi and Kanazawa that were entirely encircled by earthworks and moats.

In the case of Himezi, the outer defensive perimeter was completed by Ikeda Terumasa, who took possession of the castle after the Battle of Sekigahara in 1600. The castle town was divided by three rings of moats around the castle into the inner enclosures (*utiguruwa*) where the donjons and the residence of the lord of the domain were located, the middle enclosure (*nakaguruwa*) and the outer enclosure (*sotoguruwa*). Each enclosure was surrounded by stone walls or earthwork (*dorui*) and a moat. In Himezi, the southern portion of the earthwork surrounding the middle enclosure survives.

09 外郭（城下町）の構成－1

近世の城は、大きく全体を取り巻く**外総構**の内が、造られた城なのです。

ヨーロッパの城、中国の都城が、城壁で街を取り囲むのに対して、日本の城にはそのような構造はないと言われますが、姫路でも金沢でも見られるように、日本の城にも城下町全体を囲む土塁と水堀があります。

姫路は、西暦1600年の関ヶ原の戦いの後に入った池田輝政によって完成しました。城下町は、城を囲む三重の堀によって、天守や藩主の住まいのある内郭、内郭に近い中郭と、その外側を囲む外郭に区分されています。それぞれの郭を、石垣や土塁と、堀で囲んでいました。姫路では、中郭の南側を囲む土塁が、よく残っています。

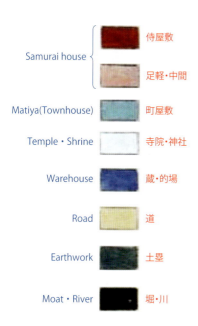

"Himezi samurai yasiki zu" (Drawing of Samurai Estates in Himezi), before 1816. (Himeji center for Research into Castles and Fortifications)

『姫路侍屋敷図』文化 13 年（1816）以前（姫路市立城郭研究室蔵）

10 The Organization of the Outer Enclosure (Castle Town) 2.

The middle enclosure of Himezi Castle was divided into large and medium-sized lots. Retainers lived in houses on lots bestowed by the domain; the size of a lot depended on the rank of the retainer. Those of low rank such as foot soldiers (*ashigaru*) lived in the outer enclosure.

Saikoku Highway (present-day National Highway 2) ran east-west through the outer enclosure. Shops were situated along this highway. The shopkeepers were merchants of the so-called *tyōnin* (urban commoners) class. Artisans, who were also of the *tyōnin* class, had their places of work in the outer enclosure as well. Temples too were to be found in the outer enclosure. In a castle town, temples often formed a community of their own referred to as a "temple district" (*tera mati*).

10 外郭（城下町）の構成－2

姫路城の**中郭**は、大きな宅地、中くらいの宅地に区分され、藩士たちが、身分に応じた規模の宅地とその土地に建つ住居を藩から給付されて、住みました。足軽など、下級の藩士たちの住まいは、**外郭**にありました。

外郭の中を、東西に西国街道（現在の国道2号線）が通っていましたので、この街道に沿って店が軒を連ねていました。街道沿いの店を営んだのは、町人の中の商人たちです。**外郭**には、町人である職人たちの仕事場もありました。**寺院**も、外郭にありました。寺院は、多くの城下町で、寺院だけの町をつくりました。そこは**寺町**と呼ばれています。（「8 姫路城図屏風」参照）

11 Earthworks and Moats around Castles

Earthworks and moats were created around castles for defensive purposes. The soil excavated in digging a moat was piled on the inner bank of the moat to form an earthwork.

There were both moats filled with water (*mizubori*) and empty moats (*karabori*). Water-filled moats were the norm, but the outer moat of Odawara Castle is said to have been left empty because its extreme length made the creation of a gradient for the flow of water impracticable.

In Himeji, an extended segment stretching east to west of the southern portion of the earthwork for the middle enclosure survives. A water-filled moat once existed on the south side of this earthwork but is now a road.

The water in the Sōgamae-bori (Defensive Perimeter Moat) of Kanazawa still flows swiftly. The moat has been narrowed, and little of the earthwork on the inner bank of the moat survives. However, the inner bank of the moat is still about a full story higher than the street on the outer bank. Though an earthwork is believed to have been built on the inner bank, people in the castle town began to tear it down and use the earth as needed from around the middle of the Edo period.

Earthwork and vestige of the moat around the middle enclosure of Himezi Castle. (The moat was located where the street and the sidewalks are now.)
姫路の中郭を囲む土塁と堀跡（堀は両側の歩道を含む道路部分）

11 城を囲む土塁と堀

　城を防御するために城下を囲んでいるのは、土塁と堀です。堀を掘る時に出る土を内側に積んで、土塁が出来るのです。

　堀には、水をたたえた水堀と水のない空堀があります。水堀が普通ですが、小田原城の外側を囲む大外郭は、延長がとても長いため水勾配をとることが出来ないので、空堀になったと考えられます。

　姫路では、中郭の南側の土塁が、東西に長く残っています。その南側に水堀があったのですが、堀は現在道路になっています。

　金沢の総構堀は、今も滔々と水が流れています。堀幅は狭められ、内側の土塁が残っているところはほとんどありません。しかし、今でも堀の内側が外側の道路面より建物1階分高くなっています。堀の内側に土塁が築かれていたと考えられますが、江戸時代の中ごろから、城下の人々が土塁の土を必要に応じて取り崩していたとのことです。

Left above：a conjectural restoration drawing of the outer defensive perimeter of Kanazawa Castle.
Left below：the present condition of the outer defensive perimeter of Kanazawa Castle.

左上：金沢城外惣構の推定復元図
左下：金沢城の外惣構の現状

Right：The parking space is where the earthwork once existed.

右：駐車スペースは、土塁があった部分と考えられる。

12 The Defensive Perimeter of Kanazawa Castle

Kanazawa Castle was built at the head of a plateau rising between two rivers, Saigawa and Asanogawa, flowing from southeast to northwest. Area names and the configuration of roads suggest that the course of Saigawa was shifted slightly to the outside when the castle was constructed.

These two rivers were made defensive lines; temple towns were located on the outside, and the earthworks and moats of the outer and inner defensive perimeters were built on the inside. A canal drew water from Asanogawa into these moats.

Called Kuratuki Canal (Kuratuki Yōsui), it feeds the moats of the outer and inner defensive perimeters. Tatumi Canal feeds the pond and fountain inside Kenroku Garden and the water that is led by stone pipe into the castle.

Today, no clear trace of the earthwork remains, but a vestige of the canal can be seen at the foot of the steps at the entrance to Oyama Shrine, the starting point for the inner defensive perimeter. The shrine precinct is approximately two meters higher than the level outside the canal.

Kanazawa Castle and its castle town in the Kanbun（1673-75）.（Isikawa Prefectural Library）
『寛文七年金沢図』の金沢城と城下町。（石川県立図書館蔵）

12 金沢城の総構

　金沢城は、東南から西北に流れる2つの川、犀川と浅野川に挟まれた台地の先端に築かれています。犀川は、築城にあたってやや外側に付け替えられたことが、町名や道路の形状などによってわかります。

　この2つの川を外側の防禦線とし、その外に寺町を配し、内には外惣構と内惣構の土塁と堀を造りました。その両構の堀に浅野川から水を引いたのが、外惣構と内惣構の用水です。

　この用水は鞍月用水と呼ばれ、外及び内の総構えの堀を流れています。兼六園の池、噴水となり、城内へ石管で導かれているのは辰巳用水です。

　現在、土塁を明確に残している所はありませんが、内惣構の始点に近い尾山神社入口階段下では、用水の名残を見ることができ、境内地は用水の外側より2メートル程高くなっています。

A drawing explaining key features shown in "Kanbun Kanazawa no zu" on the opposite page.

左ページの『寛文七年金沢図』に対する説明図（金沢工業大学増田達男研究室・金沢城調査研究所木越隆三共同研究による）

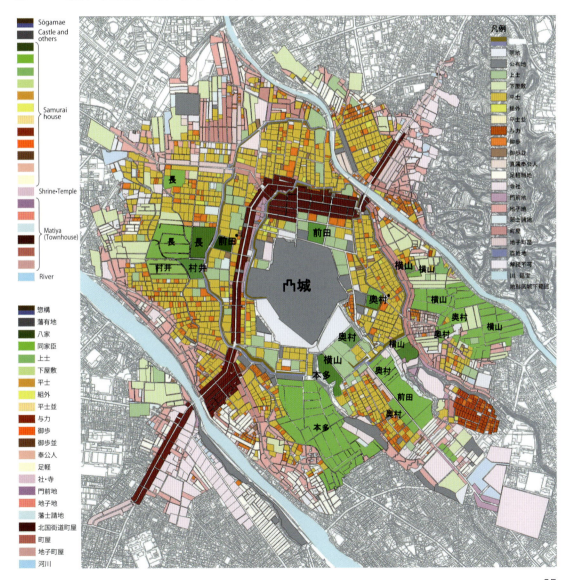

13 The Locations of Castles 1. Hill-on-the-Plain Castles

A castle constructed on a rise such as Himezi Castle was called a hill-on-the-plain castle (*hirayamaziro*). There are a number of hills in the Harima Plain, and the donjons rise on top of the highest. The hill on which Himezi Castle sits was not originally shaped as it is now. Two adjacent hills are believed to have been conjoined. The donjon on top of the hill called Himeyama affords a panoramic view of the Harima Plain. Although it was constructed at a time when Tokugawa Ieyasu had become shogun and the country was entering a long period of peace, the donjon is surrounded by three minor donjons for added protection.

The lord of the castle lived in a residence constructed in a slightly more spacious, level area just below the donjon. That was the residence of the main enclosure. Although it is believed to have been the residence of the lord of the castle at first, the residence of the tertiary enclosure functioned as such for the greater part of the Edo period.

View from the north of the donjon of Himezi Castle atop Himeyama. On the far right is the western enclosure.
北側から見た姫山上の姫路城天守郭。右端は西の丸の櫓

13 城の立地-1 平山城

　姫路城のように、小高い丘の上に造られた城を、**平山城**といいます。播磨平野の中にはいくつかの丘陵がありますが、その中で一番高い丘の上に天守が聳えています。

　姫路城の丘は、初めから今のような形をしていたわけではありません。ほとんど接するように並んでいた大小二つの丘の間を埋めて一つの丘にしたと考えられています。

　姫山の上の天守からは、播磨平野が一望できます。姫路城の天守が造られた時代は、徳川家康が将軍になり、天下が泰平に向かっていた頃ですが、天守は3つの小天守が付属する最も護りの堅い形式で造られています。

　城主は、天守のすぐ下にやや広い平らな場所をつくって、住居を建てました。それが本丸御殿です。城主は、はじめここで生活していたと考えられますが、江戸時代の大半は、三の丸の御殿に住んでいました。

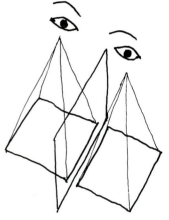

Aerial photos for seeing Himezi Castle stereoscopically. (To get a three-dimensional effect, look at the left photo with the left eye and the right photo with the right eye. The effect is more easily achieved if one stands a sheet of plastic or cardboard on the white line between the two photos.)

姫路城の立体視用の航空写真（国土地理院）。（左を左目で、右を右目で見ると立体視できる。両写真の間の白線上に下敷きなどを立てると見やすい）

14 The Locations of Castles 2. Mountain Castles

Castles in the Sengoku period (1467-1568) were so-called "mountain castles" (*yamaziro*) built atop mountains. Itizyōdani, the fortress of the Asakura clan who were wiped out by Oda Nobunaga, and Hirai Castle in Huzioka, Gumma Prefecture, are typical mountain castles. With such a castle, the castle town was constructed at the foot of the mountain.

The only mountain castle with extant buildings from the Edo period is Bittyu-Matuyama Castle (Takahasi). Its donjon is built on top of Mt. Gagyū.

At Oka Castle (Taketa, Ōita Prefecture), only the stone walls remain. Its *sangai yagura* (three-story tower), corresponding to the donjon, survived until the Meizi period and can be seen in a photograph showing the castle in its entirety.

A view from Bittyū Matuyama Castle of the castle town below (on the left bank of the river).
備中松山城から見下ろす城下町（川の左手）

14 城の立地－2 山城

　戦国時代の城は、山の上に造られた**山城**です。織田信長に滅ぼされた朝倉氏の一乗谷や、群馬県藤岡の平井城は、典型的な山城で、城下町は山の下にありました。

　江戸時代に建てられた城の中で建築遺構を残している山城は、高梁だけです。高梁では、臥牛山の上に備中松山城が築かれ、天守が建っています。

　現在、建築は失われ石垣だけがそびえているのは、岡城（大分県竹田）です。岡城では、明治まで天守に相当する三重櫓が建っていましたので、岡城の全貌を写した写真に、天守が写っています。

Oka Castle（Taketa, Oita Prefecture）. "Osiro sinkeizu."（Takeda City Board of Education）

岡城（大分県竹田市）『御城真景図』（竹田市教育委員会蔵）

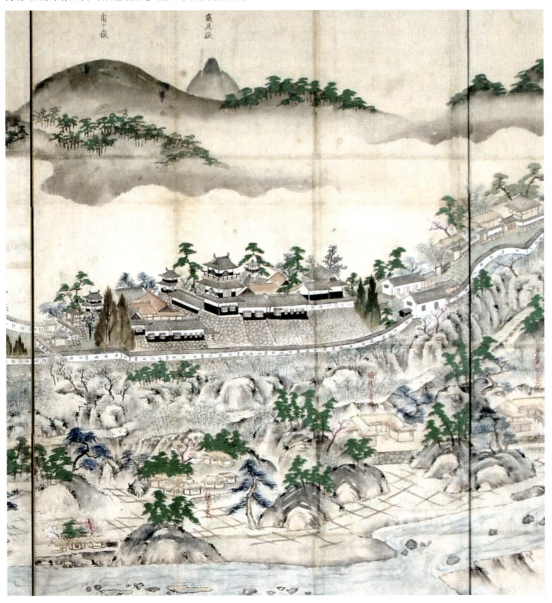

15 The Locations of Castles 3.
The Remains of Asakura Castle Town in Itizyōdani

The remains of a castle town from the Sengoku period, as well as some recreated buildings, can be seen in Itizyōdani.

The *yamaziro* was on a mountain ridge, and the town was built down below, along the Itizyōdani River. Samurai residences and the houses of artisans lined the castle town, which was bounded to the south by the earthwork for the Kaminokido (Upper Gate) and to the north by a wall of massive stones for the Simonokido (Lower Gate). The residential complex of the Asakura clan was at the foot of a hill called Siroyama near the middle of the town. The residential complex included buildings identified as the Syuden, Tunegoten, tea house, rooms for women attendants (*nagatubone*), kitchen (*daidokoro*) and stable (*umaya*). On slightly higher ground, the remains of residences with gardens called Yudono Garden and Suwa Garden have been discovered.

Samurai residences were located to the northwest, across the river. There was also the house of an artisan where bullets and prayer beads have been discovered as well as a house where a number of large pots were installed on the floor. The pots may have been used for indigo dye, but as no trace of their contents has been found, the type of trade the occupant engaged in is still uncertain.

Restored buildings of Asakura Castle in Itizyōdani. (*Left*：a district of samurai residences, *Right above*：a district of *matiya*.) *Right Below*：the remains of structures. (The white areas indicate where buildings once stood.)
一乗谷朝倉氏遺跡の復元建物（左は武家屋敷地区。右上は町屋の地区）（撮影：笠松雅弘）、右下は遺構（白い部分は建物跡の表示）

15 城の立地－3 一乗谷朝倉氏遺跡

　一乗谷は、戦国時代の城下町が、一部の建物まで再現されて、現実にみることのできる遺跡です。
　尾根の上に山城があり、一乗谷川に沿って町が作られました。城下町は、南側を区切った上城戸（かみのきど）の土塁と、北側を区切った巨大な石を積んだ下城戸の中にあり、**武家屋敷**や、**職人の家**が並んでいました。中央近くの城山のふもとに朝倉氏の館があり、館には主殿や常御殿、茶室、長局、台所、厩などと判断できる建物が並んでいました。
　一段上がったところには、湯殿庭園、諏訪庭園などと呼ばれる庭園を伴った屋敷跡も見つかっています。
　川を超えた西北側には、武家屋敷が並び、鉄砲玉や数珠玉などが見つかった職人の家や、いくつもの大きな甕を床に据えた家なども並んでいました。甕は藍染の甕と考えるのが有力ですが、中身が全く残っていないので、職種は今のところわかりません。

Overall aerial view of the remains of Asakura Town Castle in Itizyōdani. (*Itizyōdani to tyūsei tosi* (Itizyōdani and Medieval Cities))
空から見た一乗谷朝倉氏遺跡全景（30ページ右下および31ページの写真は福井県教育委員会保管）

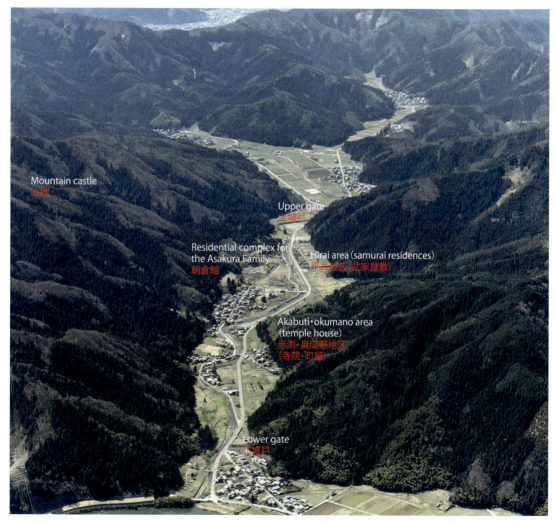

16 The Locations of Castles 4. Plain Castles

Where suitable topography was not to be found, a castle was constructed on level land with defense provided by rivers, stoneworks or moats. A castle of this type was called a plain castle (*hiraziro*).

Matumoto Castle was constructed in the early Edo period. The main enclosure was encircled by moats and stone walls on a site sandwiched between rivers, and it was there that the donjon and the residence of the main enclosure were built.

Hukui Castle also made use of land squeezed between rivers to the north and south. The donjon and residence were constructed in a main enclosure defended by several rings of moats. A number of the enclosures leading to the main enclosure had no facilities standing in them—they were simply there for defensive purposes. At Hukui Castle, the bridge over the river on the road to Kyoto begins as a solid stone structure but becomes a wooden structure halfway across. Kagaguti Gate (cf. p.89) on the north side of the castle where the road to Kanazawa began had an unusual structure. It was equipped with a "mounted exit" (*umadasi*), which concealed the departure of soldiers on horseback behind earthwork, as well as a moat.

A plain castle（donjons and the remains of the main enclosure of Matumoto Castle）.
平城（松本城の天守群と本丸跡）

16 城の立地－4 平城

　城を築くのに適した地形が得られない場合には、川や石垣、堀で防御して、平地にも城が造られました。このような城を、平城（ひらじろ）といいます。

　松本城は、江戸時代初期の築城ですが、川に挟まれた城地を堀と石垣で囲んで、本丸が構成され、天守や本丸御殿が作事されました。

　福井城も、南北を川に囲まれた地形を生かし、幾重にも堀をめぐらして、天守と御殿が築かれた本丸を防御しています。本丸に至る郭には、何の施設もない郭もあって、防御を固めていたことがわかります。

　さらに、福井城では、京への道が川を渡る橋は、途中までは頑丈な石橋ですが、残りの半分は木橋です。北側の金沢への道が城下を出るところの加賀口門（89頁参照）は、馬出しを設け、堀を廻らして護る、珍しい構造です。

Above, a plain castle sea castle (*umiziro*) (Toba Castle).
Below, a plain castle (central part of Hukui Castle) and castle town.
上：平城（海城）（鳥羽城）
下：平城（福井城と城下町の中心部分）

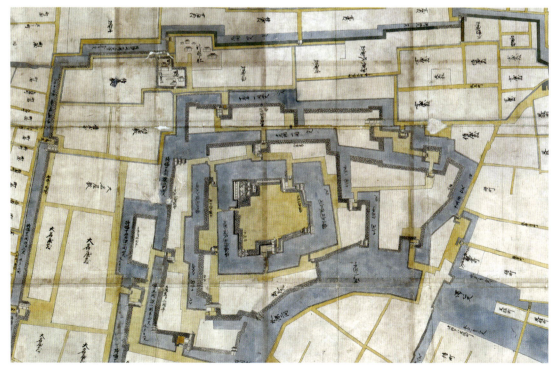

Castle and castle town of Sunpu (present-day Sizuoka City) in the Genna period (1615~1624). "Sunpu-zu" (Drawing of Sunpu). (Seikadō Library)
元和年間（1615-24）の駿府（現在の静岡市）の城と城下町『駿府図』（静嘉堂文庫蔵）

17 The Organization of Castle Towns 1.

The town that developed outside a castle's inner enclosure is referred to as a castle town. The castle town of Himezi Castle was surrounded by a defensive perimeter consisting of moats and earthworks.

The residents of a castle town were samurai, Buddhist and Shinto priests, and urban commoners (*tyōnin*, that is, artisans and merchants). Peasants lived in villages within the domain and were not permitted to live in the castle town.

Samurai Quarters   Within the defensive perimeter, the location and size of a *samurai* residence depended on rank. *Karō*, retainers of the highest rank, lived in residences closest to the inner enclosure and were given the largest lots. Low-ranking foot soldiers (*asigaru*) lived as a rule in rowhouses on the periphery of the outer enclosure.

The *samurai* quarters in the castle towns of Sumpu (Sizuoka) and Nagoya which Tokugawa Ieyasu was involved in building were laid out in grid patterns.

17 城下町の構成－1

　城の内郭を囲むように、町が出来ます。この町を**城下町**と言います。姫路城の城下町は、堀と土塁で構成された総構で囲まれています。

　城下町の住民は、武士・僧・神職、そして町人です。町人は、商人と職人です。農民は、領内各地の村に住み、城下町に住むことは許されていません。

　武家地　　総構の中で、武士の住まいは主に中郭にあり、家臣の中で最も地位の高い家老職が、最も内郭に近く、広い敷地が与えられます。身分の低い足軽は外郭の周辺の長屋に住むのが原則です。

　徳川家康がかかわった初期の城下町、駿府（静岡）や名古屋では、武家地に碁盤目状の街割りがみられます。

Samurai houses
武家屋敷

Matiya(Townhouses)
町屋

Temple
寺院

Shrine
神社

18 The Organization of Castle Towns 2.

Highways and Townhouses The main highway of the region passed through the castle town. The houses of merchants lined the highway. When there were many such houses, lots became narrower — each house had less of a frontage available for its shop — and extended further back from the street.

Artisans lived on the outskirts of the castle town.

The narrow roads of a castle town had sharp bends and T junctions. In Kanazawa, small open spaces called *hiromi* can be found at intersections all over the former castle town.

"Himezi-zyōzu byōbu" (Folding Screen with Drawings of Himezi Castle) (Siniti Ōtani)
『姫路城図屏風』（大谷信一蔵）

18　城下町の構成−2

街道・町屋　　城下町の中を、その地域の基幹となっている街道が通ります。この街道沿いに、商家が並びます。商家が多くなると、店を開く間口が狭くなり、奥行きの深い敷地が生まれます。
　職人が住んだのは、城下町の周辺部です。
　城下町の細かい道は、クランク状に折れ曲がったり、T字型になったりします。また、金沢では、広見（ひろみ）と呼ばれている交差点の広場が、城下町のあちこちに見られます。

Above, a *hiromi* in a temple district in "Enpō Kanazawa no zu" (Drawing of Kanazawa in the Enpō Era).
Below, the present condition of the same *hiromi*.
上：『延宝金沢図』の寺町の広見の部分
下：同広見の現状（上図の○印の地点から矢印の方向を見ている）

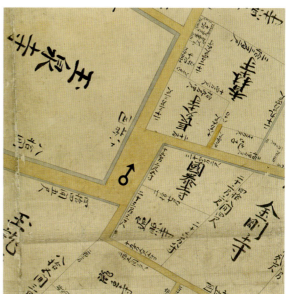

19 The Organization of Castle Towns 3.

Temple District Temples were arranged in a district of their own (*teramati*) on the highway at the boundary of the town. The temple districts of Kanazawa are located on the other side of the rivers Saigawa and Asanogawa and in the southeastern portion of the hills stretching from the castle. In the temple district on the other side of Asanogawa, each temple precinct on the mountain side is connected by an approach (*sandō*) to the Hokkoku Highway leading to Toyama. A temple district with each temple's large main hall (*hondō*) is said to have provided a line of defense for a castle town, but the temple district on the other side of Asanogawa was probably incapable of serving such a function.

Centers of the Zyōdo Sin Sect, referred to as *dōzyō*, were built not in temple districts but in various other parts of castle towns.

There were no specified locations for Sinto shrines in castle towns.

The temple district labeled ❶ in the drawing on the opposite page.
右頁の図の❶寺町部分（The grey areas are temples）

Three temple districts shown in "Enpō Kanazawa no zu."
(Ishikawa Prefectural Library)
『延宝金沢図』に見られる３箇所の寺町（石川県立図書館蔵）

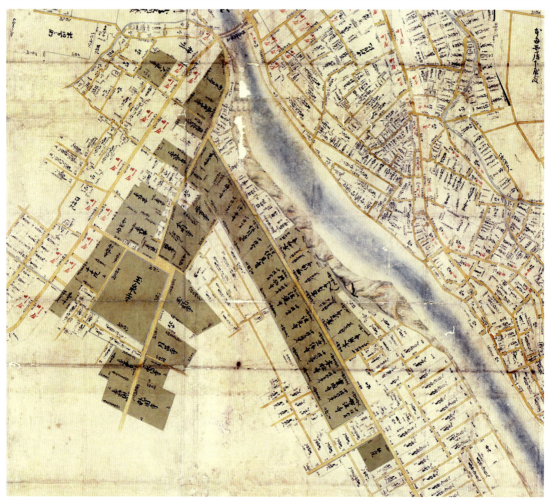

19　城下町の構成－3

寺町　　寺は、街道が町を出るあたりにまとめられ、寺町が形成されました。

　金沢の寺町は、犀川の外側❶と浅野川の外側❷と、城から続く丘陵の東南部❸にあります。浅野川の外側の寺町❷は、富山に向かう北国街道から、それぞれの寺へ参道を設けて、山側の傾斜地に境内地を配置しています。

　寺町は、それぞれの寺の本堂の規模が大きく、城下町の防衛線になるといわれますが、浅野川外側の寺町❷は、そのような役割は果たせなかったと思います。

　浄土真宗の拠点は道場と呼ばれ、寺町以外の城下町の各地に造られました。

　神社は、城下町では特に配置が定められていません。

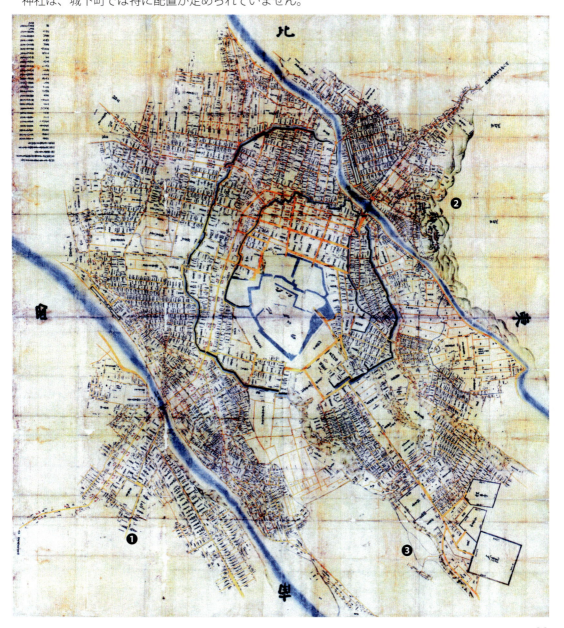

20 Enclosing a Castle Town 1.

Moats Topography and rivers were used to form lines of defense for a castle. The castle was furthermore encircled by moats. In medieval mountain castles, the ridges of mountains were cut and empty moats created because the water supply was inadequate to fill them. Moats filled with water were commonplace in castles built in the Edo period. However, even in that period, there are instances of empty moats such as the enormous empty moat that is part of the Great Defensive Perimeter (Daigaikaku) of Odawara Castle.

Takada Castle in Etigo (a province that is now Niigata Prefecture) is a plain castle encircled by water-filled moats that are bigger than those found in any other castle.

The flow of water in most water-filled moats is imperceptible, but water from the Tatumi Canal flows swiftly even now through the moat of the Outer Defensive Perimeter (Sotosōgamae) of Kanazawa Castle. (cf. page31)

Odawara Castle in its entirety. The outermost boundary is the Great Defensive Perimeter. "Bunkyū no zu（Odawara-zyō kazu）" (Drawing of the Bunkyū Era（Underdrawing of Odawara Castle））. (Odawara Castle Donjon)
小田原城の全域。一番外側を囲むのが大外郭『小田原都市集成図』（小田原市教育委員会保管）

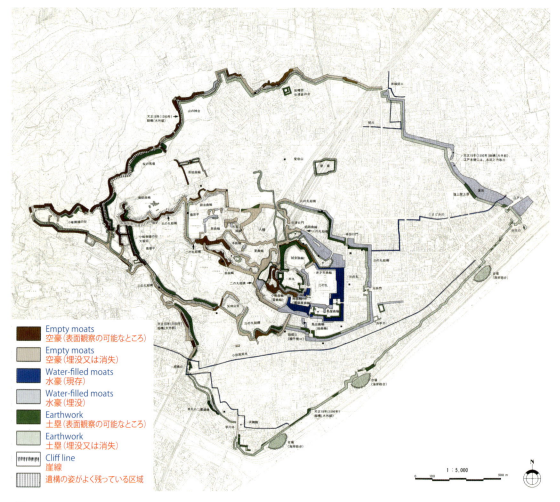

20 城下町を囲む－1

堀　城は、地形や川を利用して、防御線を形成しています。その上で、堀で囲みます。

中世の山城では、水理が悪いので、山の尾根を切った空堀が造られましたが、江戸時代の城では、堀に水を湛える水堀が普通です。しかし、中には小田原城の外の構えである大外郭のように、全く水のない壮大の空堀もあります。

平城である越後の高田城では、他の城には見られないほど、広い水堀で囲まれています。水堀は水の流れを感じないのが普通ですが、金沢城の外惣構の堀は、今でも辰巳用水の水が、滔々と流れています。（31頁参照）

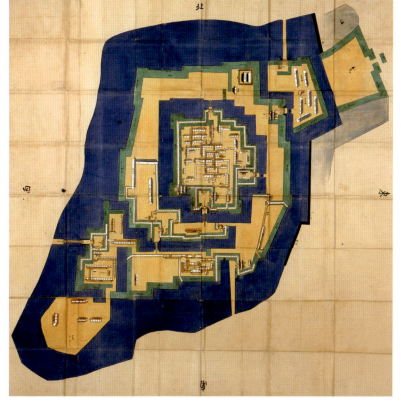

Above, inner moat and main enclosure of Takada Castle. "Takada kaifu yonhyaku nen" (The 400 Years since the Founding of Takada).
Below, Takada Castle. "Takada-zyōnai no ezu" (Drawing of Takada Castle). (Sakakibara Family historical document) The castle town lay outside the castle.

上：高田城の内堀と本丸『高田開府400年』
下：高田城『高田城絵図』（榊神社蔵）この外側に城下町が拡がる

21 Enclosing a Castle Town 2.

Earthwork Digging a moat naturally produced leftover soil. This soil was piled on the inner bank of the moat to build an earthwork. The so-called Odoi (Earthwork), constructed around Kyoto by Hideyosi, is an example from the Momoyama period (late sixteenth century). The lower half of the earthwork for the middle enclosure of Himezi Castle built in the Edo period – on the side facing the moat – is a stone wall. The earthwork of Edo Castle in the vicinity of Hanzōmon and the area between Itigaya and Iidabasi is a stone wall in both its lower section where it comes into contact with the moat and its topmost section.

There are no stone walls at all in Takada Castle in Etigo. A high earthwork encircles the main compound. Trees now grow from the earthwork but when the castle was still functioning, there was only a fence on top of the earthwork. Trees would have been a hindrance had there been any fighting. The pines and cedars are no doubt a product of a time of peace; the absence of warfare during the Edo period allowed them to grow to their present size (cf. p.22, p.41).

Earthwork and moat west of Sotosakurada Gate. (The castle is on the right side of the photo.)
江戸城外桜田門西側の土塁と堀（右側が城内）

21 城下町を囲む－2

　土塁　　堀を掘ると、当然残土が山になります。堀の内側にこの土を積んで、**土塁**を造りました。桃山時代には、秀吉が築いた京の御土居のような例があります。江戸時代に築かれた姫路城の中郭の土塁は、外側の堀に面する側の下半分を**石垣**としています。

　江戸城の半蔵門のあたりの土塁や、市ヶ谷から飯田橋の区間に見ることができる土塁は、堀に接する下部と最上部を石垣としています。

　越後の高田城では、全く石垣がありません。高い土塁が、本丸を囲んでいます。江戸城も高田城も今は土塁に樹木が茂っていますが、城が機能していた時代には、土塁の上にあったのは塀だけで、戦闘の際に邪魔になる樹木はなかったはずです。平和の世になって、松や杉が育ったのでしょう。江戸時代には平和が続いたので、大きな木に育ちました。（姫路城 22 頁、高田城 41 頁参照）

Earthwork and moat of Edo Castle's defensive perimeter.（The earthwork was leveled in the middle to lay the JR Tyūō Line tracks.）

江戸城外構の土塁と堀（土塁の中間を平らに削って JR 中央線が走る）

22 Enclosing a Castle Town 3.

Stone Walls In Himezi Castle, an earthen embankment rises from the moat on the north side of the inner enclosures; only at the very top does it become a stone wall. However, the walls inside the inner compounds are basically stone.

Kumamoto Castle is well known for its high, solidly-constructed stone walls. Some of those walls were built when Katō Kiyomasa was lord of the castle while others were constructed by the Hosokawa clan. Beneath the residence of the main enclosure, stone walls built in the Katō era and those built when the castle was expanded in the Hosokawa era overlap, and the difference in slope is quite apparent.

The stone walls of Himezi Castle and Kanazawa Castle were often expanded or relaid in the Edo period, resulting in obvious differences in appearance.

The two stone walls below the main enclosure of Kumamoto Castle. (*Right*, the Katō-era wall ; *left*, the Hosokawa-era wall.)
熊本城本丸下の二重の石垣（右が加藤時代、左が細川時代）

22 城下町を囲む−3

　石垣　　姫路城では、内郭の北側には、堀から立ち上がる自然のままの土手の上に石垣を築いていますが、内郭の内は、基本的には石垣を築いています。

　高く、堅固な石垣としてよく知られているのは、熊本城です。

　熊本城には、加藤清正時代に築かれた石垣と、細川氏の時代になって築かれた石垣とがあります。本丸御殿の下では、加藤時代の石垣と細川時代に拡張した時の石垣が重なっていて、勾配の違いがよくわかります。

　姫路城でも、金沢城でも、江戸時代にしばしば拡張や積直しが行われたので、その違いを観察することが出来ます。

Isikawa Gate, Kanazawa Castle.（*Above*, Isikawa Gate and wall ; *below*, the view of a *masugata* from within a *yaguramon*.）
金沢城石川門（上：石川門と太鼓塀、下：櫓門の内から枡形の石垣をみる）

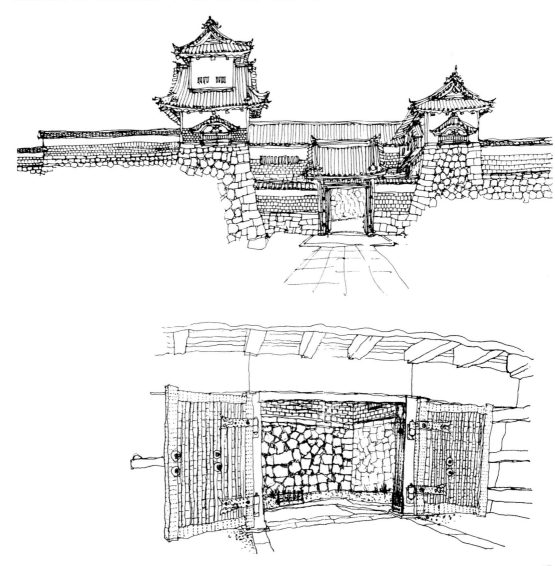

23 Laying Stone Walls 1.

Cutting and Transporting Rocks   The quarries at Kanazawa Castle and Matumae Castle have also been designated historical sites. That is because rocks that have been hewn roughly to size and wedge holes dug for the purpose of extracting rocks as well as fragments left from the shaping of rocks remain in those places where rocks were excavated and cut. The rocks were transported from the quarries to the castles on carts and sleds.

A rock used in a stone wall was two or three times longer in the transverse direction than it was on the face. The slope or curve of a stone wall was adjusted by wedging small stones behind rocks. In Kanazawa Castle, steel clamps were inserted where slight adjustments were necessary.

River gravel was packed behind the rocks visible on the wall surface. This was referred to as "back filling" (*uragome*). Two pieces of stone shaped into rectangular form with the year and month the stone wall was built inscribed on them have been discovered in the back filling of the stone wall on which the Gozyukken Yagura (Fifty Bay yagura, a long narrow building) of Kanazawa Castle once stood. This is similar to the practice of attaching a "ridge plate" (*munahuda*) on which the date of construction and other information were written on the ridge beam of a building.

A large rock pulled down a slope on a sled. "Isi-biki zu." (Izumikan)
傾斜地で修羅にのせた大石を引きおろす。『石曳図』（和泉館蔵・箱根町立郷土資料館提供）（欠損部分を補筆）

23　石垣を積む－1

石を切る、石を運ぶ　　金沢城や松前城では、石切り場も史跡に指定されています。それは、石を取り、切った場所に、今も石垣のためにおおよその形を整えた石や、石を切り出そうと開けた矢穴が残っている石や、石を成形したときの破片を見ることが出来るからです。

石取り場から城までの長い道のりを、台車に乗せるか、修羅に乗せて運びました。

石垣の石は、奥の方向に表面の2～3倍の長さがあります。石の後部に小さな石を噛ませるなどして、石垣の勾配や曲面を調整しています。金沢城では、微調整が必要なところでは、鉄製の鎹を挟んでいました。

表に見える石の後ろには、小さな川原石が詰め込まれます。裏込めと言います。金沢城の五十間櫓の石垣では、裏込めの中から、直方体に成形され、表面に石垣を築いた年月を刻んだ2個の石が見つかりました。建築でいえば、棟札に当たるようなものです。

A large rock being loaded on two boats arranged side by side. "Isi-biki zu."
大石を2艘並べた舟にのせる。『石曳図』

24 Laying Stone Walls 2.

Building Stone Walls   The way rocks were shaped and finished was distinctive to each castle, but there were broadly speaking three different ways stone walls were laid. The oldest technique used in feudal castle-building was *nozura-zumi*. Naturally found stones such as river stones were piled, unworked aside from their exposed surfaces which were made more or less even.

Next, there was *utikomi-hagi*. The sides where a rock came into contact with other rocks, as well as its exposed surface, were hewn roughly into planes before piling. Small stones were inserted into gaps between rocks.

The last technique to be developed was the *kirikomi-hagi*. Not only was the exposed surface made even but the entire rock was worked so that there were no gaps between it and adjacent rocks.

At a corner of a wall, rocks laid on one side meshed with rocks laid on the other. The technique of alternating courses to form a corner was called *sangi-zumi* and appears to have come into use around the start of the Edo period.

"Tikuzyō zu byōbu"（Folding Screen with Drawings of a Castle under Construction）.（Nagoya City Museum）.

石垣を積む。足場を作って石を積む様子。『築城図屏風』（名古屋市博物館蔵）

Above：A stone wall being laid. The scene shows scaffolding being assembled and stones being laid
Middle：Back filling being toted.
Below：Stones for a stone wall being carried on carts and pulled using rope.

上：足場を作って石を積む
中：裏込石を運ぶ
下：石垣の石を車で運ぶ、縄をかけて引く

24 石垣を積む－2

石垣を築く　石垣は、石の形や表面の仕上げに、それぞれの城で違いがあり、特色となっています。石垣の積み方の特色は、おおまかに3つに分けられます。

その一つが、野面積。河原の石などを使い、表面部分を平らに欠くだけで、ほとんど加工せずに積む手法です。近世の城づくりでは、一番古い手法です。

その次が、打込はぎ。表面をおおよそ平らにするだけでなく、石と石が接する面もおおよそ平面に加工して積み上げています。積んだとき隣の石との間にできた隙間に小さな石を詰めています。

最も新しいのが、切込はぎ。表面を平面に仕上げるだけでなく、隣の石との間に隙間がなくなるように加工しています。

石垣の隅は、両側から積まれてきた石を組み合わせています。互い違いに両面の石を組む積み方を、算木積といいます。算木積が使われるようになるのは、江戸時代に入るころのようです。

Examples of different ways of laying stone walls. *Left*：*nozura-zumi*, *Middle*：*utikomi-hagi*, *Right*：*kirikomi-hagi*.
石垣の積み方の例、左：野面積　中：打込はぎ　右：切込はぎ

25 Laying Stone Walls 3.

A stone wall flares out toward the bottom, a feature intended to increase stability. Not only that, it usually follows a concave curve in the middle. It thus forms an arch, fixed by the ground below and a structure such as a tower on top, that counteracts the pressure on the stone wall from within.

A stone wall may form an arch not just in section. In the early feudal period, each side of the stone wall on which a structure such as the donjon sat arched inward at the top, so that the wall in plan resembled a spool. The stone wall of the donjon of Maruoka Castle is an example.

Where the ground was weak, the base of the stone wall was widened to increase the area of support. At times, wooden piles were driven into the ground to support a stone wall. In the case of Matumoto Castle, two logs were placed in parallel, and two other logs were placed in parallel at right angles to the first pair; the bottom rocks (*neisi*) of the stone wall were arranged on top of those logs. While immersed in water, wooden piles or logs will not rot; they will continue to support rocks.

Rocks may be placed or small stones packed in front of the *neisi* to prevent those bottom rocks from being pushed out.

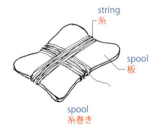

Stone wall of the donjon of Maruoka Castle.
Left：plan. The wall is spool-shaped at both the top and the bottom.
Right：a small lean-to roof covers the space between the top of the stone wall and the building proper.

丸岡城天守の石垣。
左：平面図。上面も下面も糸巻状になっている。『日本建築史基礎資料集成』
右：石垣上面と建物の間に小屋根を架けている。

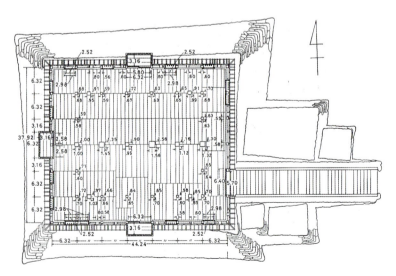

25 石垣を積む－3

　石垣は、安定のため、下ほど広がっています。それだけでなく、中ほどが内にはいる曲面が普通です。石垣の中からの圧力を受けるので、下は地面、上は櫓などの建築物で押さえられた、アーチにしているのです。

　断面がアーチ状であるだけでなく、近世初期の石垣では、上から見たときに天守などが乗っている石垣の上面の各辺を、内側にアーチ状にし、上面全体が糸巻状になっています。丸岡城の天守台石垣は、その例です。

　地盤が弱いときには、石垣の裾を広くして、支える面積を広げています。ときには、木の杭を打って石垣を支えたり、松本城のように丸太を井桁に組んでその上に根石（石垣の一番下の石）を据えています。木の杭や丸太は、水の中にある間は腐らず、いつまでも石を支えています。

　根石が前に押し出されないように、根石の前に石を置いたり、小石を詰めたりしている場合もあります。

The ground underneath the stone wall of the donjon of Matumoto Castle. *Matumotozyō syūri hōkokusyo* （Report on the Repairs of Matumoto Castle）.

松本城天守台石垣下の地形『国宝松本城（解体・調査編）』

26 The Facilities of a Castle Town 1. Guard Stations

Gates, Guard Stations A castle town was encircled and protected by rivers, moats and earthworks. To control movement in or out, a gate (*kido*) was installed where a highway or a road from a nearby village crossed a line of defense. In a large city such as Edo, a stone wall with a gate manned by guards was built on a highway and referred to as a *mituke* or an *ōkido*. In addition, a fence, gate, and guard station (*ban'ya*) manned by a gate guard (*kidoban*) were installed at every intersection between different districts (*mati*) of the *tyōnin* (urban commoners) quarters. The guard checked all traffic between about ten at night when the gate was closed and about six in the morning when the gate was opened, opened a side gate to let people through and sent word ahead to the next guard station. The gate guard was employed by the district and lived in the station. The wages were so low that, to get by, guards engaged in trade as well, as is depicted in the *Kidaisyōran* (Excellent Views of a Brilliant Era).

Yotuya Ōkido（Yotuya Gate）of Edo. "Edo meisyo zue"（Guide to Famous Edo Sites）.
江戸の四谷大木戸『江戸名所図会』

26 城下町の施設－1　番所

木戸、番所　城下町は、周囲を川や堀、土塁等で囲んで防御していましたので、街道や周辺の村からの道がその防衛線を越えるところに木戸を設けて、出入りを規制していました。

江戸のような大都会では、街道の出入り口に、石垣を築き、門を造り、番人を置いて、見付或は大木戸と呼んでいました。そのうえ町人地では、町境の辻ごとに、柵と木戸と番屋を設け、木戸番を置いていました。

夜、10時ころに木戸を閉めたのちは、朝6時ころに木戸を開けるまで、木戸番が通行人を改め、木戸の潜り戸を開け閉めして、次の番屋に申し送る制度でした。木戸番は、町が雇い、この番屋に住み込んでいました。木戸番の給料が安かったため、熈代照覧に描かれた江戸の番屋では、商売をしている様子が見られます。

Gate and guard station for the gate guard in the *tyōnin* quarters of Edo. "Kidaisyoran"（Museum of Asian Art, Berlin）
江戸町人地の木戸と木戸番の番屋『熈代照覧』（Ⓒ bpk/Museum für Asiatische Kunst, SMB/Jürgen Liepe/distributed by AMF）

27   The Facilities of a Castle Town 2. Fire Watchtowers

Fire Watchtowers   Fire watchtowers (*hinomi yagura*) are to be found everywhere in bird's eye views of Edo. They are also often found in depictions of samurai residences in a genre of paintings called *doroe* and of urban scenes in woodblock prints.

There were roughly three types of fire watchtowers in Edo. One was the fire watchtower for a *samurai* residence, supported on four posts that leaned in toward each other; the structure was entirely covered with boards painted black. A second, the district fire watchtower, had the same structure but boards covered only its top half. There were also simple watchtowers erected on the top of roof ridges.

Simpler still was the ladder with a fire bell hung on top that served as a fire watchtower for a guard station (*zisinbansyo*).

Fire watchtowers were commonplace in the Edo townscape—reflecting the frequency of major fires in Edo—but were less conspicuous in other castle towns.

A guard station at an intersection and a fire watchtower on a rooftop. "Gyōnin-zaka kazi emaki" (Gyōnin-zaka Fire Scroll).
辻番所と屋根の上の火の見櫓『行人坂火事絵巻』

27 城下町の施設－2 火の見

　火の見櫓　　江戸の町を鳥瞰的に描いた絵を見ると、あちこちに火の見櫓が立っているのが目につきます。泥絵に描かれた武家屋敷や、浮世絵の町の絵にも、しばしば火の見櫓が見られます。

　江戸の火の見櫓は大別して3種あり、一つは、4本の柱を上に行くほど狭めて立て、全体に板を貼り黒く塗った武家の火の見櫓。同じ構造で、上半分ほどだけ板を貼った町の火の見櫓。屋根の棟の上に、物見台の様に組んだ簡単な火の見台がありました。

　さらに簡単なのは、梯子を立て、上部に半鐘をつっている自身番所の火の見です。

　江戸はしばしば大火に見舞われたので、多くの火の見櫓が江戸の景色を作っていましたが、ほかの城下町については、火の見櫓がそれほど目立って描かれた町はないようです。

Left above, the fire watchtower for a samurai residence. "Gyōnin-zaka kazi emaki."
Left below, a district fire watchtower. "*Edo meisyo zue.*"
Right, a fire watchtower built on top of the roof ridge of a *matiya*. "Edo-zyō kazi emaki"（Edo Castle Fire Scroll）.

左上：武家屋敷の火の見櫓『行人坂火事絵巻』
左下：町の火の見櫓『江戸名所図会』
右：町屋の棟の上につくられた火の見櫓『江戸城火事絵巻』。その上に梯子を立てて火事の様子を見ている。

28 The Facilities of a Castle Town 3. Water Supply 1.

Water Supply   Wells were the main supply of water for everyday use.

Seaside castle towns undertook the development of waterworks because their well water contained salt.

Edo could not depend on wells, much of it being on reclaimed land, and waterworks began to be installed early in its history. The first such project was the Kanda Waterworks, which drew its water from Inokasira Pond. Subsequently in 1654, water from the river Tamagawa was drawn by an open channel to Yotuya Gate (Yotuya Ōkido); there, after treatment, it was diverted into stone, wood and bamboo pipes and distributed underground in the city. The area name Suidōbasi (literally "Water Supply Bridge") came from the fact that a bridge was built alongside a wooden aqueduct used to convey water over the moat.

Water for the main enclosure and the western enclosure of Edo Castle was conveyed over the moat by copper pipe below Kitahane-basi (North Drawbridge) into a *masugata*-type gate and used to supply drinking water and feed the garden pond.

Ōarai Dam located below Meziro Plateau. *Edo meisyo zue*.
目白下大洗堰 『江戸名所図会』

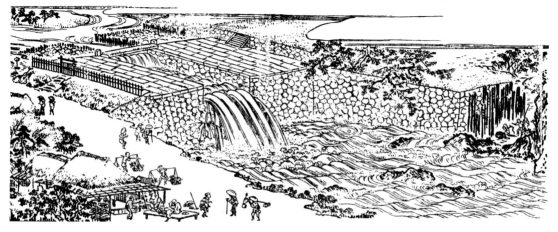

28 城下町の施設−3　水道−1

　水道　　生活用水は、主に井戸で賄われました。
　海辺の城下町では、井戸水も塩分を含んでいるので、上水道が計画されています。
　江戸では、海を埋め立てた土地も多く、井戸に期待ができなかったので、早くから上水道が敷設されています。そのはじめは神田上水で、井の頭池を水源としています。
　その後、1654（承応3）年に、多摩川の水が四谷大木戸まで開渠で引かれ、大木戸のところで調整されたのち、石樋、木樋、竹樋と分岐され、暗渠で市中に配られました。
　水道橋の名は、堀を橋のように見える木樋で堀を渡っていた懸樋に並んで橋のかけられたためにつきました。その様子は浮世絵にも描かれています。
　江戸城本丸や西の丸などの中にも、銅樋を使って導かれ、北桔橋下で堀を渡り、枡形門内に引き入れられて、飲料水や、庭園の池などに使われました。

Kanda Waterworks pipe spanning the moat at Otyanomizu in the foreground；Suidōbasi is in the background. *Edo meisyo zue*.
お茶の水の神田上水懸樋（手前）、水道橋（奥）『江戸名所図会』

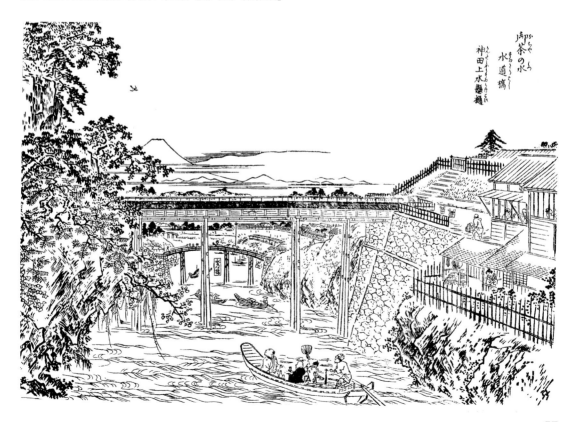

29 The Facilities of a Castle Town 4. Water Supply 2.

The water supply terminated in wells where water was stored to be drawn up with pails.

In Edo, many urban commoners lived in rowhouses which were also served by the water supply. There was a community space among the rowhouses with a well, outhouses and a place for garbage collection.

Water drawn from the community water supply or purchased from a seller of water was stored in a large pot for use in the kitchen of a rowhouse.

Waste water from the kitchen of a rowhouse was drained, via a sink on the entrance floor into a covered sewage ditch built into the middle of the passageway serving the rowhouses.

Communal well, outhouses and place for garbage collection for back-street rowhouses. "Tosiotoko kogane no mamemaki."
裏長屋の共同の井戸、後架、芥溜 『歳男金豆蒔』

29 城下町の施設-4　水道-2

　水道の末端は、井戸の形式で水が貯められ、桶でくみ上げていました。
　江戸では、町人たちの多くが長屋に住んでいましたが、長屋にも水道が引かれていました。長屋の中に設けられた共同の場所に、井戸形式で汲む水道のほか、共同の便所（後架）や芥溜がありました。
　長屋の台所では、大きな甕に水を溜めて使っていました。その水は、共同の水道から汲んできたり、水売りから買ったようです。
　長屋では、台所で使った排水は、入口の床に作られている下流しを経て、長屋内の通路の中央に設けられた下水溝（板で蓋がしてある）に流されました。

Depiction of the entrance to back-street rowhouses（showing a covered sewer ditch）. "Ukiyo-doko."
裏長屋への入口（板で蓋された下水溝が描かれている）『浮世床』

30 The Facilities of a Castle Town 5. Theaters

Theaters   Theaters (*sibaigoya*) for Kabuki plays were built in the feudal period in Edo as well as Kyoto. At first, the stage was similar to a Nō stage, and the audience area was roofless. However, two tiers of boxes eventually came to be built around a level seating area, which too came to be roofed. The stage, which until then had had its own roof like a Nō stage, was stripped of this feature around Kansei 8 (1796) in the well-known Nakamura and Itimura Theaters in Edo.

The stage was equipped with a revolving stage (*mawaributai*) and a trapdoor (*seri*).

Extant Kabuki stages of this kind are Kanamaru Theater in Kotohira, Yatiyo Theater in Yamaga, and Kureha Theater preserved in Meizi-mura.

Castle towns were enlivened by performances in not only permanent theaters but makeshift playhouses.

30 城下町の施設－5　芝居小屋

　芝居小屋　　歌舞伎芝居の芝居小屋は、近世にはいると、京をはじめ、江戸にもつくられました。初めのころは、能舞台のような**舞台**と、屋根のない観客席でしたが、次第に平土間の観客席を囲んで周りに二階席が設けられるようになり、平土間にも屋根がかかるようになります。よく知られている江戸の中村座や、市村座などは、寛政8年（1796）に舞台にあった能舞台のような屋根がなくなります。

　さらに、**舞台**には回り舞台や迫（せり）が設けられます。

　このような歌舞伎舞台の様子は、琴平にある金丸座や、山鹿の八千代座、明治村に保存されている呉服座にみることができます。
くれはざ

　城下町では、常設の劇場もありましたが、仮設の芝居小屋でも興業が行われ、賑わいました。

Left page："Nakamura-za naigai no zu" (Drawing of the Interior and Exterior of the Nakamura Theater in Sakai, Edo). (National Diet Library).

左ページ：『中村座内外の図』（国立国会図書館蔵）

The roofs colored burnt sienna are theaters. "Edo hitome" (Bird's Eye View of Edo).

茶色の大きな三角屋根が芝居小屋『江戸一目』。

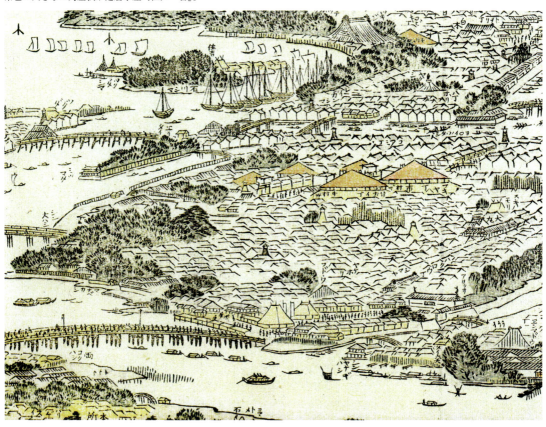

31 The Facilities of a Castle Town 6. Bath Houses

Bath Houses A bath house (*huroya*) is depicted in a picture drawn in the Edo period on the skirting of a *syōzi* screen from the audience hall (*taimenzyo*) of the residence of the main compound (*hommaru goten*) in Nagoya Castle. The bath house consists of a small steam bath enclosed by boards and a room floored with boards where people wash themselves. There are no bathtubs.

The *yuya* was a facility where people soaked in hot water and then washed themselves in a room floored with boards. It is not certain when the *yuya* became commonplace, but in *Morisada mankō*, a nineteenth-century encyclopedia, under 'Edo bath houses (*yokuko*),' a plan is shown in which men and women are segregated; it is explained that separate bathtubs have traditionally been provided for men and women in Edo. Material from the Bunka era (early 1800s) also refers to such facilities as *huroya*, *yuya* and *sentō* and states that there were more than 600 of them in Edo.

The *yuya* probably came to be called *huroya* when a wall that came halfway down from the ceiling began to be built to contain steam from a bathtub and create the effect of a steam bath.

A drawing of the layout of the Higasi Tyaya district in Kanazawa shows a bath house (*yuya*) at the entrance to a *hiromi* (open space).

Right Page Above right: Layout of a *yuya* in Edo, "Morisada mankō." *Above left*: the entrance to the steam bath and large bathtub. "kengu irigomi sento sinwa"
Below: Men's bath, "Ukiyo-buro.

上右：江戸の湯屋の平面図『守貞漫稿』　上左：浴槽のある奥の小屋の入口。（ざくろ口という）『賢愚漆銭湯新話』
下：男湯の様子『浮世風呂』。左上に風呂の入口であるざくろが描かれている。

Community bath house depicted on the lower part of a *syozi* in the audience hall of the residence of the main enclosure, Nagoya Castle. "Hūzokuzu" (Administrative Office, Nagoya Castle).
名古屋城本丸御殿対面所の障子の腰に描かれた町の風呂『風俗図（風呂屋）』（名古屋城総合事務所蔵）

31　城下町の施設－6　湯屋　風呂屋

　湯屋　江戸時代の初めに描かれた名古屋城本丸御殿対面所の障子の腰に描かれた絵に、風呂屋の様子が描かれています。風呂屋は、板で囲われた蒸し風呂の小部屋と、体を流す板の間から構成されていて、後の湯屋のような湯船は備えていません。

　湯屋は、湯船の湯につかり、上がって板の間で体を洗い流す形式の施設です。いつごろから湯屋が一般的になったのか確かなことはわかりませんが、『守貞漫稿』には、「江戸浴戸」として男女を分けた平面図を載せ、江戸は従来より男と女の湯船を分けていた、と書いてあり、文化年代のころ（1800年代の初めころ）の資料では、風呂屋、湯屋、銭湯とも言い、江戸には600軒余あったと書いてあります。

　湯屋を風呂屋というようになったのは、湯船の前に垂れ壁を設けて蒸気を溜め、蒸し風呂のような形になったからでしょう。

　金沢の東茶屋街の江戸時代の町割り図を見ると、入り口の広見（広場）に湯屋があることがわかります。

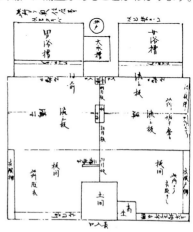

32 The Development of the Feudal Castle 1.

Himezi in the Kuroda Kambei Period (1567-1573)   In the major repair of Himezi Castle undertaken in the Syōwa era (1926-89), a smaller foundation (*tensyudai*) was discovered inside the foundation. In addition, many old items were discovered among the material used in the western minor donjon. The report written at the time of the repair speculates that these were from the donjon built by Hasiba Hideyosi.

Ordered by Oda Nobunaga to attack the Mōri clan, Hideyosi built a new castle in Himezi where Kuroda Kambei had earlier constructed a castle. However, as he had only limited time available, the foundation and the old items in the western minor donjon discovered in the Syōwa-era repair project may well have been from the donjon of the Kuroda Kanbei period.

Recent studies have gradually made clear which parts were built by Asano Nagamasa after he took charge of construction. Further investigations will undoubtedly throw light on the appearance of the castle in the Kuroda Kambei period as well.

Conjectural restoration of the donjon of Himezi Castle built by Hideyosi.（Himezi City）.
秀吉が建てた姫路城天守の推定復元模型（姫路市蔵）

32 近世の城が出来るまで－1

黒田官兵衛時代の姫路　姫路城では、昭和の大修理の時に、天守台の中から一回り小さな天守台が見つかっています。また、西小天守の材の中に、多くの古材が見つかり、報告書は、それらは秀吉が築いた天守の古材であろうとしています。

秀吉は、信長に命ぜられた毛利攻めに際して、黒田官兵衛の城のあった姫路に、新たな城を築きました。しかし、時間も限られていましたから、昭和の大修理で見つかった天守台と、西小天守の古材は、黒田官兵衛時代の天守のものという見方もできると思います。

近年の調査で、浅野氏が入場してから普請した部分が少しずつ分かるようになってきましたから、調査が進めば、官兵衛時代の様子もわかるようになることでしょう。

Survey of foundation stones of the Hideyosi-period donjon excavated from within a stone wall under the ground floor of the main donjon of Himezi Castle.（according to the Report）.
姫路城大天守の地階床下の石垣内から発掘された秀吉時代の天守の礎石群の実測図（『姫路城保存修理工事報告書』による）

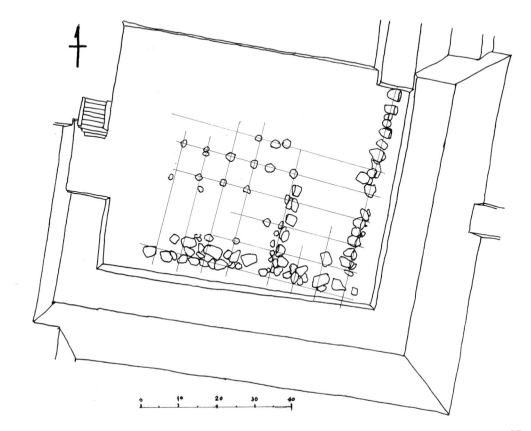

33 The Development of the Feudal Castle 2.

Himezi Castle since the Asano Period   The oldest plan showing everything inside the outer enclosure is the *Himezi osiro mawari samurai yasiki sin'ezu* ("New Plan of the Samurai Estates Around Himezi Castle" cf. p.36) which has been passed down in the Sakakibara family. This plan shows that townhouses (*matiya*) lined the highway. A folding screen with a painting of Himezi Castle (in the possession of Mr. Sin'iti Ōtani of Etizen City) depicts people coming and going on a street of townhouses roofed in tiles and boards weighed down with stones.

There are folding screens depicting castles towns all over Japan. They show the distinctive quality of townhouses in each castle town. There is one from the late Edo period showing both banks of the Saigawa in the vicinity of the bridge called Saigawa Ōhasi in Kanazawa. The highway across the bridge is lined with shops including a fish store, and a carpenter is shown working on another street.

Townhouses (matiya). "Himezi-zyō zu byōbu." (Siniti Ōtani).
町屋 『姫路城図屏風』（大谷信一蔵）

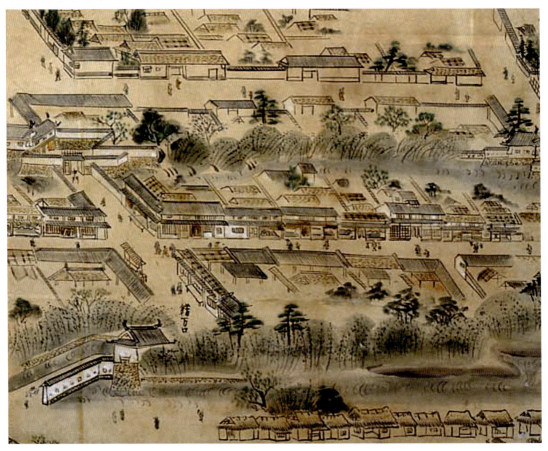

33　近世の城が出来るまで−2

浅野時代以後の姫路城　　外郭内すべてを描いた絵図は、榊原家に伝えられた『姫路御城廻侍屋鋪新絵図』(36頁参照)が最も古く、この図では、街道沿いは町屋であったことがわかります。姫路城図屏風には、瓦葺や石置き屋根の町屋の通りを行き交う人々が描かれています。

各地の城下町を描いた屏風が残っています。それぞれの城下町の町屋の特徴がわかります。

金沢には、江戸時代後期に描かれた、犀川大橋近辺の両岸を描いた屏風があります。犀川大橋を渡る道は北国街道です。犀川大橋を渡った街道には、魚屋をはじめとする店が並び、二筋裏では表の道で作業している大工が描かれています。

Saigawa Ōhasi and the townhouses on the side closer to the castle. "Kanazawa-zyōkazu byōbu." (Isikawa Prefectural Museum of History). The street on the far right is the carpenters' district.

犀川大橋とその内側の町屋『金沢城下図屏』(石川県立歴史博物館蔵)
一番右の通りが大工町

34 Constructing a Castle 1. Location

The place a castle was built depended on the purpose it was meant to serve. Deciding on the location of a castle was referred to in books of military strategy as *zidori* (seizing land). For example, Oda Nobunaga whose objective was to secure control over the entire country, sought to prevent the Mōri, the leading clan in the western part of Honsyū from advancing on Kyoto and force the Mōri to submit to him. Himezi Castle was conceived as the linchpin in his strategy with respect to western Japan. A castle built by Kuroda Kambei already existed in Himezi, but Hasiba Hideyosi, Nobunaga's leading general, took over and remade it.

Tokugawa Ieyasu, who eventually became shogun, attempted to contain powerful *tozama daimyō* (who were not his hereditary vassals and might in the future turn against the Tokugawa family). For example, he placed Yūki Hideyasu, his second son, in Hukui and Matudaira Tadateru, his sixth son, in Takada, to the west and east respectively of Kanazawa, the seat of the Maeda clan.

The relative locations of western Japan, Himezi and Kyoto.

西国と姫路および京の関係

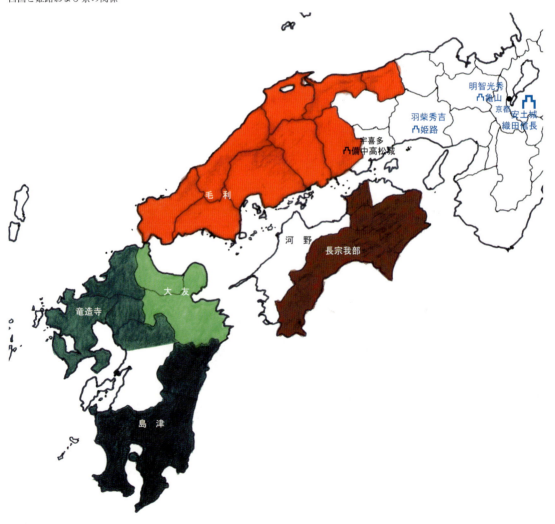

34 城の構成－1　地選・地取り

　城を設ける場所は、その城をどのような目的で造るかによっています。城の場所を決めることを、軍学書では、「地選」、「地取り」といっています。例えば、姫路城は、全国制覇を図った織田信長にとって、中国地方の雄毛利氏が京へ上るのを阻止し、毛利氏を服従させることを意図して、西国に対する要として築かれました。姫路にはすでに黒田官兵衛の城がありましたが、先鋒の羽柴秀吉が受け取り、作り直したということです。

　また、将軍になった徳川家康は、将来将軍家に敵対しないとは限らない有力な外様大名を封じ込めることを意図しています。例えば、金沢の前田家に対して、西は二男結城秀康を福井に、東は高田に六男松平忠輝を配しています。

The relative locations of Kanazawa, Takaoka and Toyama, ruled by the Maeda clan, Hukui, ruled by Yūki Hideyasu, and Takada, ruled by Matudaira Tadateru. The red line is the route taken by the Maeda clan in complying with the rule of *sankin kotai* (alternate attendance).

前田の金沢、高岡、富山に対する結城の福井、松平の高田の関係、赤線が前田家の参勤のルート

35 Constructing a Castle 2. Site Plan

Once the location of the castle was decided, the arrangement of the enclosures and the locations of the moats to be dug and the earthworks to be built were determined. This was referred to in books of military strategy as *nawabari* (rope stretching).

Various types of *nawabari* have been identified including the *rinkaku*-type, in which the main enclosure in the middle was surrounded by concentric enclosures, and the *teikaku*-type, in which a succession of enclosures was built outside the entrance to the main enclosure, but these classifications are taken from Edo-period books of military strategy or the result of research into castles since the modern era. They were not guiding principles but reflect the analysis of actual castles.

In reality, conditions were different for each castle. There was no hard-and-fast rule for how advantage might be taken of existing topographical features or how such features might be altered, for example, by connecting or carving hills and changing the course of rivers.

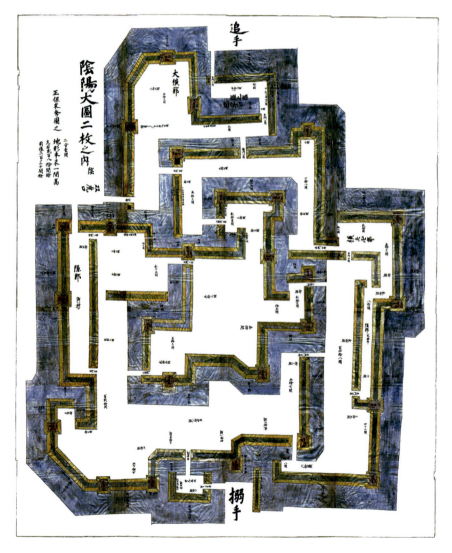

35 城の構成−2 縄張り

　城を造る場所が決まると、郭の配置を決め、堀を掘り、土塁や濠をめぐらす、設計をすすめることになります。この行為を、軍学書では**縄張り**といっています。

　縄張りは、中心の本丸を囲むように、四方に広げていくものを輪郭式、本丸の虎口の外側に次々と郭を設けるものを梯郭式などと分類していますが、これは、江戸時代の軍学書や、近代以降における城郭研究の結果による分類で、設計に際しての指針というよりは、実例を集約し分類した結果ということが出来るでしょう。

　実際には、丘陵や川などの地形の条件をどのように生かし、或いは丘陵を繋げ、削ったり、川を付け替えるなど、城によって条件はそれぞれ違っています。

Left page：Form of *nawabari* shown in an Edo-period book of military strategy.
左ページの図：江戸時代に軍学によって作られた縄張りの一形式

Western-style *nawabari* at Goryōkaku（Hakodate, Hokkaido）, dating from the end of the shogunate.
幕末の西洋式縄張りの五稜郭

36 Constructing a Castle 3. Constructing a Donjon 1.

In the case of one donjon-1. The oldest extant donjon is that of Maruoka Castle (Hukui Prefecture), a hill-on-the-plain castle; only the donjon survives in a main enclosure built on slightly high ground. Steps leading directly to the entrance of the donjon are attached to the outside of the stone walls. The donjon sits on a foundation built using the *nozura-zumi* technique. A wooden pent-roofed area fills the gap between the donjon and the top of the foundation. (cf. p.50, p.80)

In the case of one donjon-2. In both Edo Castle and Osaka Castle, a small foundation of some size was attached in front of the entrance to the donjon. In neither case was a small donjon ever built on top of that small foundation.

In the case of one donjon-3. The entrance, which was difficult to defend in the case of a freestanding donjon, was enclosed. In the extant donjon of Matsue Castle (Simane Prefecture), an attached tower (*tuke-yagura*) was built outside the entrance.

In the case of one donjon-4. The entrance of the donjon of Inuyama Castle is built in a stone base. There, the stone wall protrudes beside the entrance and an attached tower was built. This tower afforded a good view of the entrance and enabled defenders to attack any enemy soldiers converging there. (cf. p.80)

Left：a freestanding donjon. Donjon of Maruoka Castle（Sakai, Hukui Prefecture）. *Right*：a freestanding donjon. Donjon of Edo Castle, "Edo-zu byōbu."（National Museum of Japanese History）
左：独立天守。丸岡城天守（福井県坂井市）　右：独立天守。江戸城天守『江戸図屏風』（国立歴史民俗博物館蔵）

36 城の構成−3　天守の構成−1

天守 1 基の場合− 1　現存する天守のうちで、最も古い丸岡城天守（福井県）は平山城で、小高い本丸に天守だけが残っています。天守への階段が石垣の外に一直線に付き、天守の入口に向かいます。天守は野面積の天守台の上いっぱいに建っていますが、石垣の上面が整形でないので、石垣の周りと天守の隙間に木造の小屋根をかけています。（50 頁、80 頁参照）

天守 1 基の場合− 2　江戸城天守や、大坂城天守のように、1 階に設けた大天守の入口の前に、ある程度の広さを持った小天守台を付けている場合があります。江戸城でも大坂城でも、小天守台に小天守が建つことはありませんでした。

天守 1 基の場合− 3　独立した天守では、入口を防御するのが難しいので、入口を囲うことになります。現存する松江城天守はその例で、入口の外側に付櫓を設けています。

天守 1 基の場合− 4　犬山城の天守の入口は石垣にあります。この天守では、入口の横に石垣を張り出して、付櫓を設けています。この付櫓からは入口がよく見え、入口へと集まった敵を攻撃することが出来たでしょう。（80 頁参照）

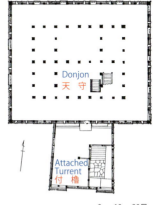

Freestanding donjon. The donjon of Matue Castle（Matue, Simane Prefecture） with an attached tower built at the entrance.
Right：plan. *Below*：donjon. In the foreground is the attached tower over the entrance.

独立天守。入口に付櫓を設けた松江城天守（島根県松江市）
右上：平面図　下：天守。手前は入口の付櫓

37 Constructing a Castle 4. Constructing a Donjon 2.

In the case of two or more donjons   Matumoto Castle started with two connected donjons, and an attached tower (*tuke-yagura*) and the so-called Tukimi Tower were subsequently added to arrive at the present form. In the original scheme, the donjons looked down on an entrance in the stone wall beneath the corridor (*watari-yagura*) that connected them.

Himezi Castle has four connected donjons.

In Matuyama Castle, where as in Himezi, the courtyard is surrounded by corridors connecting the donjon and three towers, the entrance to the courtyard is under a corridor connected to the donjon and the entrances to the structures including the entrance to the donjon are either in the stone wall of the donjon or in towers connected to the donjon by corridors.

A group of four connected donjons is said to be the the soundest form of donjon from a defensive point of view. In light of the fact that this form developed after Tokugawa Ieyasu took control of the country, however, its aim in all likelihood was to be impressive and aesthetically pleasing.

Donjons of Matumoto Castle. *Left* : minor donjon. *Right* : main donjon.
松本城天守。左：小天守　右：大天守

37 城の構成−4　天守の構成2

天守2基以上の場合　松本城天守は、はじめ2基の天守をつなぐ形であったものが、後さらに付櫓および月見櫓が加わって現状になりました。最初の形は、両天守を繋ぐ渡櫓下の石垣にある入口を、両側の天守から見下ろす形式です。

姫路城の天守は、4基の天守が連立する形式です。

4基の天守が連立する天守群は、最も護りの堅い形式と言われますが、このような天守群ができたのが徳川家康が天下を取った後という時期であることから考えると、4基の天守が並び立つ連立天守群の力強さ・美しさが、大きなねらいだったと思います。

姫路城と同様に天守と3基の櫓をつなぐ渡櫓で中庭を囲む松山城では、中庭への入口が天守につながる渡櫓の下にあり、天守などへの入口は、天守の石垣と、天守に渡櫓でつながる櫓にあります。

Himezi Castle, with its four connected major and minor donjons.
(*Foreground*：northwestern minor donjon. *Right*：western minor donjon. Rear：main donjon. *Left*：eastern minor donjon)

四基の大・小天守が連立する姫路城天守
（手前：乾小天守、右：西小天守、奥：大天守、左：東小天守）

38 Constructing a Castle 5. Constructing the Donjons of Himezi Castle

Constructing the donjons of Himezi Castle   Himezi Castle has one main donjon and three minor donjons, and these are connected by two-storied structures called *watari-yagura*. The three minor donjons are referred to by their positions as the western minor donjon, the inui (northwestern) minor donjon and the northern minor donjon.

There is a gate in the *watari-yagura* connecting the main donjon to the western minor donjon. one can go through this gate, pass under the western minor donjon and arrive at the courtyard. The entrances to the donjons from the courtyard are on the ground floor of the main donjon and on the ground floor of the *watari-yagura* connecting the western minor donjon and the northwestern minor donjon.

A kitchen (*daidokoro*) stands in the courtyard. There is another kitchen on the ground floor of the main donjon.

Inside the main donjon, there are no rooms with a particularly identifiable function other than the kitchen and the lookout.

Originally there were to be windows all around the top floor of the main donjon. However, during construction, the end bays were installed with thick panels and became plastered walls on the outside. The reason for this change is not clear, but perhaps it was decided to create walls at the four corners and reinforce the structure from the weight of the roof. If the floor had been built without the corner walls, it would have afforded a splendid 360-degree view.

Entrance to the group of donjons of Himezi Castle. Kitchen in the courtyard of the donjon group. Plan.
姫路城天守群への入口。同中庭の台所　平面図　→大天守への経路

38 城の構成－5　姫路城の天守の構成

　姫路城の天守群は、大天守と3棟の小天守から構成され、その間を、二階建ての渡櫓が繋いでいます。3棟の小天守は、その位置によって、西小天守、乾（北西）小天守、東小天守と呼ばれています。

　大天守と西小天守をつなぐ渡の下に門があり、この門から西小天守の下を通って中庭に出ます。天守群への入口は、この中庭に面する大天守地階と、西小天守と乾小天守を結ぶ渡櫓の地階にあります。

　中庭には、台所が建っています。台所は、大天守の地階にもあります。大天守の中は、台所と最上階の望楼のほかには、特に使用目的がわかるような部屋はありません。

　大天守最上階の周囲は、すべて窓として計画されたのですが、工事の途中で、隅の柱間に厚い板をはめ、外を漆喰塗とした壁に変わりました。なぜ改造したかはわかりませんが、屋根の重みから、四隅に壁を作って補強したのかもしれません。もしこの壁なしに出来上がっていたら、最上階からの360度の眺めは、見事だったことでしょう。

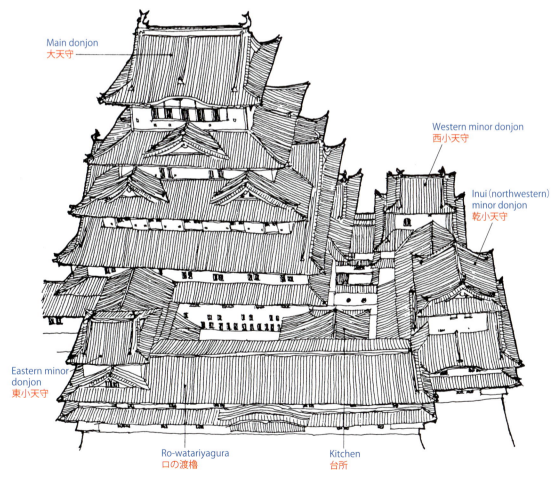

Connected donjons of Himezi Castle.
姫路城の連立式天守群

39 The Structure and Design of Donjons and Towers 1.

Towers Buildings for defensive purposes in a castle were called *yagura* (towers).

The biggest and most symbolic *yagura* in a castle were called *tenshu* (donjon). As a rule the shogunate in the Edo period only permitted the construction of *yagura* that were three-storied at most. As a consequence, in many of the castles built in the Edo period, the tower corresponding to the donjon was a three-story *yagura*.

Besides the donjon, one-, two- and three-story towers were built in strategic places in a castle.

Even the long, narrow buildings constructed along stone walls were a type of *yagura* called *tamon-yagura*.

Tenbin Yagura (Scale Tower) of Hikone Castle (Hikone, Siga Prefecture).
彦根城の天秤櫓（滋賀県彦根市）

39 天守・櫓の構造と意匠−1

　櫓　　城を構成している防御的な建物を、櫓と呼んでいます。
　城内で、最も規模の大きい象徴的な櫓を、天守と呼んでいますが、江戸時代には、幕府が、原則的に、三重の櫓までしか建てることを許さなかったので、江戸時代に整備された多くの城では、天守に相当する櫓を三重櫓としています。
　天守の外、城の要所に一重、二重あるいは三重の櫓を建てています。
　石垣に沿って長く連なる建物も櫓の一種で、多聞櫓と呼んでいます。

Uto Yagura（Uto Tower）, main enclosure of Kumamoto Castle.

熊本城本丸宇土櫓

40 The Structure and Design of Donjons and Towers 2.

The first donjon took the form of a lookout set on top of the roof of a tower (*yagura*). The donjon of Maruoka Castle is an example. The donjon of Inuyama Castle started out as a two-story tower, to which a lookout was later added on top.

Next, one two-storied tower was built on top of another to create a still larger form of donjon. This resulted in two layers of large hip-and-gable (*irimoya*) roofs on the outside. Being simply a lookout, the top floor did not need to have a semi-gabled roof; instead, it became a monitor with a hipped (*yosemune*) roof. However, the large hip-and-gable roofs continued to be necessary until the top of the stone foundation became a regular rectangle in form and it became possible to reduce the plan of each successive floor in equal measure on all sides.

To avoid the large gable of a hip-and-gable roof, a form of roof developed called the paired wing hip-and-gable (*hiyoku irimoya*) roof, in which the gable was split into small gables added at the corners, one to the right and one to the left. Both the large gable of the hip-and-gable roof and the paired wing hip-and-gable roof became unnecessary when the gradual diminution of the plan was achieved. Donjon roofs were subsequently ornamented with one fairly large dormer gable (*tidorihahu*) in the middle or two small dormer gables, one to the right and one to the left.

Left: South elevation of the donjon of Maruoka Castle (Sakai, Hukui Prefecture); *Right*: south elevation of the donjon of Inuyama Castle (Inuyama, Aiti Prefecture).
左：丸岡城天守南面立面図（福井県坂井市）　右：犬山城天守南面立面図（愛知県犬山市）『日本建築史基礎資料集成』

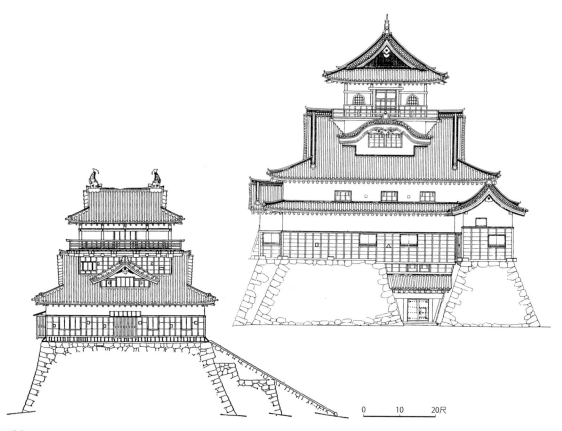

40 天守・櫓の構造と意匠－2

　天守は、櫓の屋根の上に物見の望楼を載せたのが最初の形です。丸岡城の天守は、その例です。犬山城の天守は、最初2階の櫓が造られ、後に屋根の上に望楼を載せて完成しました。

　さらに規模が大きくなると、2階建ての櫓を2段重ねる形で発展します。そのため、外観に大きな入母屋の屋根が2度重なる姿が見られます。上層の屋根は、屋根の上に望楼を載せるだけなので、必ずしも入母屋にする必要がないために、寄棟の腰屋根に変わりますが、下の層の大きな入母屋の屋根は、石垣上面が整形の長方形になり、その上の階の平面が4面ともに同じだけ逓減するようになるまで、必要でした。

　大きな入母屋の破風を避けるために、比翼入母屋という、入母屋の破風を左右の隅の小さな破風に分けた形式が生まれました。大きな入母屋の破風も、比翼入母屋形式も、平面の逓減が整うと必要がなくなります。その後は、意匠として、真ん中に大きめな千鳥破風1つ、あるいは隅棟から離れて、左右に小さな千鳥破風が2つ付く形に変わります。

Above：paired wing hip-and-gable roof of the main donjon of Edo Castle. Two dormer gables. （National Archives of Japan）
Middle：paired wing hip-and-gable roof of the main donjon of Himezi Castle.
Below：large hip-and-gable roof of the main donjon of Himezi Castle.

上：江戸城大天守の千鳥破風2つ（国立公文書館蔵）　中：姫路城大天守比翼入母屋破風
下：姫路城大天守の大入母屋破風

41 The Structure and Design of Donjons and Towers 3.

The lookout on the top level was encircled originally by a veranda with a balustrade but eventually enclosed by a white plastered wall without a balustrade.

There is a balustrade around the top floor of the donjon of Hikone Castle. However, one must step over the sill of the cusped arch windows (*katō mado*) to get out onto the veranda, and there is not even enough headroom to stand. The protruding roof of the floor below interrupts the veranda, making it impossible to circle the veranda completely. The veranda is ornamental and of no practical use. This is the most elaborately designed donjon extant, from the point of view of the arrangement and design of the gables and the ornamentation on the ridge and the window frames. This is the ultimate example of the form of donjon in which the lookout was set on top of the tower roof.

With the disappearance of the veranda on the top floor and the achievement of the gradual and regular diminution of floors, it became possible to adopt the monitor form for all roofs other than the roof over the top floor. The form became clear but also simple and absent of any distinguishing character.

Elevation of the donjon of Hikone Castle（Hikone, Siga Prefecture）.
彦根城天守（西南）面（滋賀県彦根市）

41 天守・櫓の構造と意匠－3

　最上層の望楼部分は、周囲に勾欄付の縁をめぐらしていましたが、勾欄のない白土塗の塗籠壁に変わります。

　彦根城天守は、最上階に縁を廻らしていますが、火灯窓の敷居を超えないと縁に出られませんし、出ても軒に頭がぶつかります。縁は下の層の屋根で切れていて、一回りすることが出来ません。実用性はなく、装飾です。破風の配置や意匠、大棟や窓枠の装飾を含め、現存天守の中で最も凝った意匠の天守です。櫓の屋根の上に望楼を載せた天守形式の最後の姿です。

　最上階の縁がなくなり、下層が規則的に逓減するようになると、最上階の屋根以外のすべての屋根が、腰屋根形式でよくなります。形は明快になりますが、単純な形になって個性が乏しくなります。

Elevation of the donjon of Tuyama Castle. (Restoration by Mitio Huzioka).
津山城天守立面図（復元：藤岡通夫）

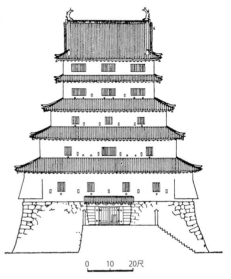

Kokura Castle Scrall
小倉城絵巻

A section of the main donjon of Himezi Castle.

姫路城大天守断面図

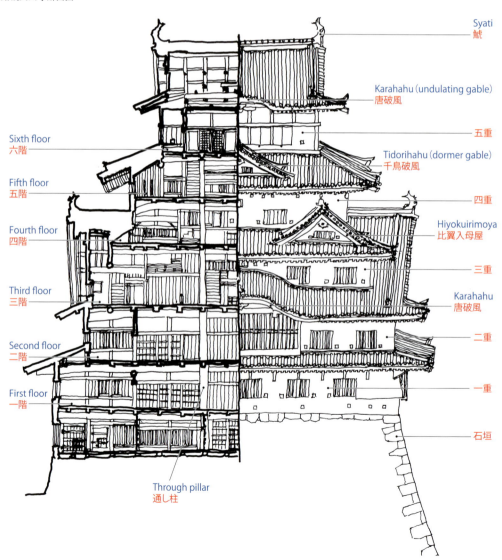

42 The Structure and Design of Donjons and Towers 4.

Donjons and Towers with Central Pillars (*Simbasira*)

The structure of the donjon of Himezi Castle is also organized around two large pillars, east and west, that reach all the way to the top floor. The east pillar is one tall trunk that goes from a base stone under the ground floor to the top floor, but the other consists of two trunks that have been tenoned together to accommodate a beam.

Seven two-story towers once surrounded the donjon of Ueda Castle. Each of the three existing towers has a central pillar reaching from a stone base set on earthwork to a beam on the top floor. Base stones remain where the central pillars ought to have stood in the other towers, suggesting that all seven structures had the same structure organized around a *simbasira*.

42 天守・櫓の構造と意匠－4

心柱のある天守・櫓

姫路城の天守では、最上階の床下までの東西2本の大柱が構造の中心になっています。東の1本は、地階の床下の礎石から最上階の床下まで届く長い柱ですが、もう1本は、梁を組んでいくときの必要性から、途中で継がれています。

上田城の本丸には7棟の二重櫓がありました。現在立っている3棟は、ともに中心に土塁上の礎石から最上階の梁に達する1本の心柱があります。ほかの櫓の残っている礎石にも、心柱の位置に礎石がありますから、7棟すべて心柱を持つ同じ構造であったと考えられます。

Plans and section of the west tower, Ueda Castle.
上田城本丸西櫓平面図および断面図

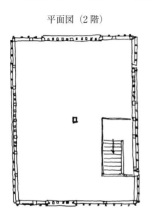
平面図（2階）

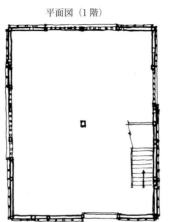
平面図（1階）

断面図

43 The Structure and Design of Donjons and Towers 5.
Yazama, *Teppōzama*, *Isiotosi*

Yazama* and *Teppōzama Round or rectangular openings in donjons, towers and walls were loopholes for shooting arrows and firearms.

Tall, narrow rectangular holes were arrowports (*yazama*); the openings were larger in cross-section on the inside to provide archers with greater flexibility in aiming arrows.

Square or round openings were gunports (*teppōzama*). Some gunports were in fairly low positions, enabling musketeers to fire from a prone position.

Isiotosi Another type of defensive device installed in donjons, towers and walls was the stone-drop (*isiotosi*). It was usually located in a tower or fence above a stone wall in order to strike at enemy soldiers climbing the wall. A stone-drop afforded a good view of the stone wall directly below and appears to have been a credible means of defense. However, a stone dropped from its narrow opening was not guaranteed to hit an attacker squarely. Since a stone wall flared out in a curve, a dropped stone that hit the wall would have caromed off it at a nearly horizontal angle and undoubtedly struck one or possibly more attackers.

The lower portions of castle walls in the West were also curved for the same reason. Whether this idea was conceived by the Japanese independently or based on a Western model is as yet uncertain.

Plan and elevation of an *isiotosi* and a section of a *teppōzama* (Matsumoto Castle).
石落しと鉄砲狭間の断面図及び正面図（松本城）

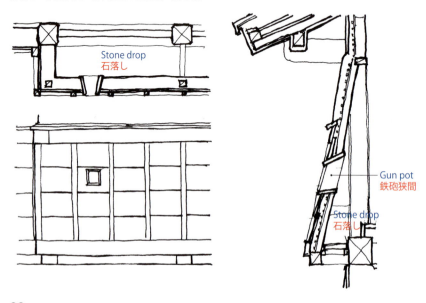

43　天守の外観構成と意匠－5　矢狭間　鉄砲狭間　石落し

矢狭間・鉄砲狭間　　天守や櫓、塀にあいている丸や四角の穴は、矢を射るため、鉄砲を構えるための穴です。

穴の中で、縦に長い長方形の穴は、矢を射るための矢狭間で、穴は内側の方が広くなっています。弓につがえた矢の、狙える角度が広くなるような工夫です。

正方形と丸い穴は、鉄砲を構えるための鉄砲狭間です。鉄砲狭間には、かなり低い位置にあけられているものがありますが、これは伏せた姿勢で鉄砲を撃つ場合のものです。

石落し　　もう一つ、天守や櫓、塀に設けられている攻撃用の装置に、石落しがあります。石落しは、通常石垣の上の櫓や塀に設けられています。石垣を登って来る敵を攻撃するための装置です。確かに、石落しから下を見ると、石垣の面がよく見えて、なるほどと思います。しかし、幅の狭い石落しから、石垣を登って来る敵を狙って石を落しても、命中するとは限りません。石垣は外へカーブして張り出していますから、上から落した石は、石垣に当たれば必ず跳ね返ります。跳ね返った石は、水平に近い角度で飛ぶので、石垣下に雲霞のごとく押し寄せてきた敵の誰かに当たるでしょう。一人だけでなく、何人かを倒すことができたかもしれません。

この考えは、西洋の城も、同じ考えで城壁の上部に石落しを設けています。戦闘の時だけ木造のはり出しを作ることもありました。石落しがヨーロッパの城の仕組みをまねたのかは、今のところわかりません。

Left, Isiotosi (Matumoto castle)
Right, A turret of the fortress of Carcassonne. The wooden projection is the stone-drop.

右、松本城の石落し
左、カルカソンヌ城（フランス）の櫓。木造で張り出しているのが石落し

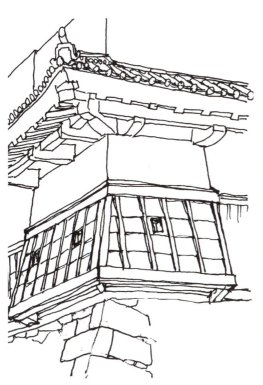

44 The Facilities of a Castle 1. Gates 1.

The forms of gates used in a castle were *yaguramon*, *kōraimon* (in Edo Castle, this form of gate was called *kabukimon*), *munamon*, and *uzumimon*. In addition to these gates, gates called *heizyūmon* and *kabukimon* were also used in the castle residence.(cf. p.90, 91)

To solidify the defense of the entrance to the castle, a *kōraimon* and a *yaguramon* were combined with stone walls topped with a *tamon-yagura* or fence to form a square, enclosed court (*masugata*). In a *masugata*, the *kōraimon* was usually situated on the outside, and the *yaguramon* on the inside of the castle, but there are examples such as Utunomiya Castle where the *yaguramon* is on the outside and the *kōraimon* is on the inside.

A *yaguramon* was a *tamon-yagura* with a stone wall at either end and double doors opening inward in the middle. The doors were built with many vertical ribs and surfaced with horizontal boards; a bolt was installed on the inside. A single wicket door was often installed, either in one of the doors or to the side of a pillar. The following gates had the same structure.

A *kōraimon* had double doors (their lower halves often covered with boards) opening inward installed between the two main pillars. A beam called the *kabuki* spanned the two main pillars, and a gabled roof with its ridge at right angles to the direction of entry was arranged on top. A secondary pillar stood behind each main pillar, and a gabled roof was arranged between each main pillar and its secondary pillar.

Left: the *masugata* of Isikawa Gate, Kanazawa Castle, *Right*: Toneri Gate, a (restored) *kōraimon* of Hukui Castle.
左：金沢城石川門の枡形　右：福井城舎人門の高麗門（復元）

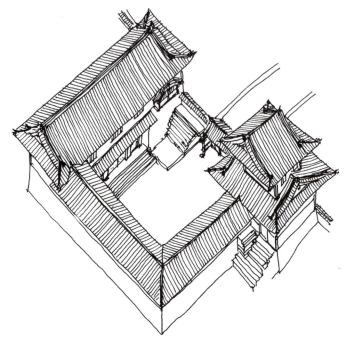

44 城の施設－1　門－1

　城に使われる門の形式には、櫓門、高麗門（江戸城の場合には高麗門の形式の門を冠木門と呼んでいました。）、棟門、埋門があります。城内の御殿では、これらの形式のほかに、塀重門、冠木門も使われました。（90、91頁参照）

　城の入り口を固めるために、高麗門と櫓門を組み合わせ、二つの門とその上に多聞櫓や塀を載せた石垣で方形の広場を囲んで、枡形をつくりました。枡形では、堀を渡った表側に高麗門、城内側に櫓門を作るのが一般的ですが、宇都宮城のように、外側に櫓門、内側に高麗門を配する例もあります。

　多聞櫓の下の石垣を両端だけとし、中央に内開きの観音開きの扉を付け、入口とした門を櫓門といいます。扉は、縦の桟を多く入れ、表面に横に板を貼り、内側に閂を設けます。多くの場合、片開きの潜り扉を、片方の扉に設けるか、主柱の脇に設けます。扉の構造は、高麗門でも同じです。

　高麗門は、2本の主柱の間に内開きの観音開きの扉（下半分に貼る例がしばしば見られます。）を付けます。主柱に冠木と呼ぶ梁を渡し、さらに上に平入りの切妻屋根をかけます。主柱の内側にそれぞれ控柱を立て、主柱と控柱の上にも切妻屋根を懸けた門の形式です。

View from without of the *umadasi* and *kōraimon* of Kaga-guti Gate, Hukui Castle.（Ekki bunko）

外側から見た福井城加賀口門の馬出しと高麗門。『福井城郭各御門其他見取絵』（越葵文庫蔵）

45 The Facilities of a Castle 2. Gates 2.

Heizyūmon   The two main pillars for the gate were erected in an opening in a fence. This type of gate was equipped with inward opening double doors.

Yakuimon   This was similar to the *kōraimon* but did away with the roofs between the main pillars and their secondary pillars; the ridge was displaced halfway between the main pillars and the secondary pillars and a gabled *hirairi* roof (a roof whose ridge was at right angles to the direction of entry) was arranged on top.

Munamon   This was a form of gate without secondary pillars, where the main pillars were covered with a gabled *hirairi* roof. It was equipped with inward opening double doors.

Uzumimon   A side gate installed in an opening in a stone wall or fence, it was equipped with inward opening doors.

Sikyakumon   This gate with a gabled hirairi roof had secondary pillars both in front of and behind the main pillars.

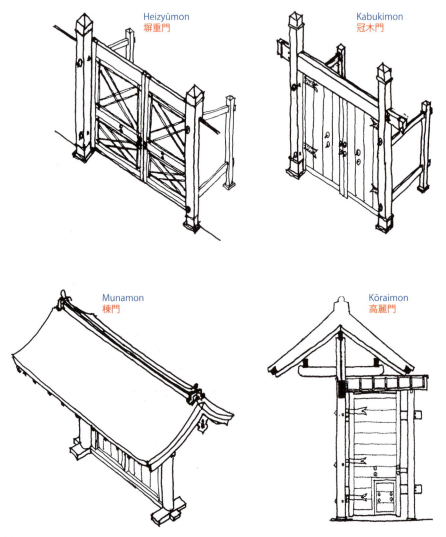

45 城の施設−2 門−2

塀重門　塀を切って2本の主柱を立てた門。主柱の内側に控え柱を設けます。内開き観音開きの扉をつけます。

冠木門　2本の主柱に冠木を設けた門。主柱の内側に控え柱を設けます。内開き観音開きの扉をつけます。

薬医門　控柱との間の屋根をやめるため、屋根の棟を主柱と控柱の間にずらし、切妻平入りの屋根だけにした門。

棟門　主柱の上に切妻平入りの屋根を懸けた、控柱のない形式の門。内開き観音開きの扉をつけます。

埋門　石垣にあけた穴あるいは塀に設けた潜り門。内開きの扉をつけます。

四脚門　主柱の前後に控柱を立て、平入りの切妻の屋根をかけた門。御殿の門として使われます。

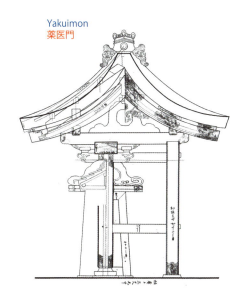

Yakuimon
薬医門

Uzamimon
埋門

45-2

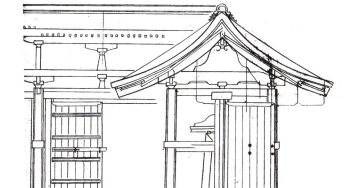

Sikyakumon
四脚門

Sikyakumon
四脚門

46 Building Construction Work 1. *Husin* and *Sakuzi*

To build a castle, the proper topography was chosen and the *nawabari* or site plan determined. Decisions were made decided where to locate the main enclosure and build the donjon, and where to arrange secondary, tertiary and other enclosures to protect the main enclosure. Each school of military strategy had its own distinctive way of arranging and forming enclosures.

Once the site plan was decided, defensive facilities such as two- and three-story *yagura*, corridor-like *tamon-yagura* and earthen walls were arranged. Decisions also had to be made about how to build the residence and facilities of entertainment such as a tea house for the lord of the castle, the place of work for carpenters, plasterers and other artisans, and storehouses for weapons and foodstuffs.

In the Edo period, civil engineering works and works such as the construction of stone walls performed in service of the site plan were referred to as *husin*. The work of constructing buildings such as donjons and residences was called *sakuzi*. Though by no means clear-cut, a distinction was made in the use of these terms.

In the architectural vocabulary of the Edo period, there was no major difference between different clans (*han*) or between samurai class or the nobility in the thickness of posts or the dimensions of members such as the *sikii* and *kamoi* (respectively the lower and upper runners) used in buildings, for example, *goten* (palatial residences). Slight differences did exist in the thickness of posts. The technique of determining through proportion the dimensions of members or the distance between members, based on the thickness of the post, was called *kiwari-zyutu*. The technique of drawing shapes such as the curve formed by the eaves was called *Kiku-zyutu*.

An example of *kiwari-zyutu*.

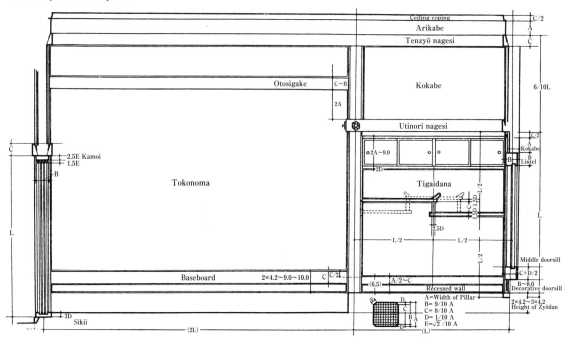

46 建築工事－1　普請と作事

　城を作るには、地形を選んで、城の原型である**縄張り**を定めます。どの部分を本丸として天守を建てるか、本丸を守るために、二の丸、三の丸などの郭をどのように配置するか、を定めていきます。兵法によって、郭の配置や形に特徴があります。

　縄張りが定まると、二重・三重などの櫓や廊下状の多聞櫓、土塀など防禦施設を配置するとともに、城主の住まいや茶室などの遊びの施設、大工・左官その他の仕事場、武器や食料などの倉庫などをどのように設けるかなどを決めます。

　江戸時代の用語では、縄張りを実現するための土工事や石垣工事などを、**普請**といいます。天守や御殿を建てる建築工事を、**作事**といいます。これらの用語の使い方は、厳密ではありませんが、区別されるのが普通です。

　また、江戸時代の建築では、御殿のように、藩が違っても、武家でも公家でも柱間隔の基準寸法は全く同じです。また、建物に使われる柱の太さや、敷居・鴨居など部材の寸法に大きな相違がありません。多少の違いは、柱の太さにありました。部材や部材間の寸法を柱の太さをもとに比例で定める方法を、**木割**術といいました。また、軒のそりなど形を製図する方法を、**規矩**術と呼んでいました。

木割の例

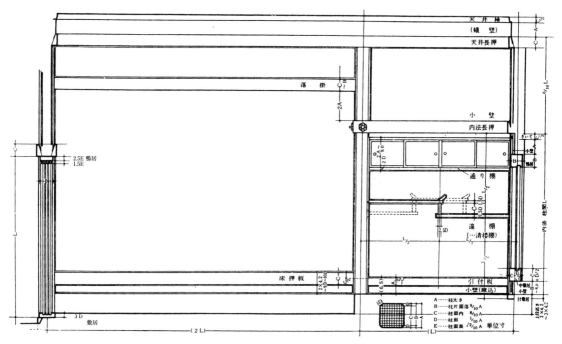

47 Building Construction Work 2. Architectural Drawings 1.

Diverse drawings were prepared when a building was to be constructed even in the Edo period. The basic one was the *sasizu*, in which the plan of the building was drawn on the entire site to show the overall arrangement. The scales most often used were *nibu-kei*, in which one *ken* was reduced to two *bu*, *rokubu-kei*, in which one *ken* was reduced to six *bu*, and *issun-kei* in which one *ken* was reduced to one *sun*. One *ken* was equal to six *syaku* and five *sun*; one *syaku* was equal to ten *sun* or one hundred *bu*. That meant the *nibu-kei* was 1:325; the *rokubu-kei* was 6:650 or approximately 1:108; and the *issun-kei* was 1:65.

Hari-ezu To prepare a drawing, a mount large enough to cover the entire site was first made out of white paper, and a grid, with lines spaced half-*ken* apart, was drawn with a spatula. The plan was white in the Keichō era (1596-1615) at the start of the Edo period and pale blue from around the Genna era (1615-1624). In the Kan'ei era (1624-1644), buildings were shown in pale blue, and the veranda (*engawa*) around them was in yellowish-brown color. From around the Meireki era (1655-1568), different colors came to be used to distinguish roofing materials and floors. From around 1700, the grid began to be drawn using black or red lines. The plan of each building was prepared on a separate paper, cut out, and pasted on the mount.

Kaki-ezu From around 1700, plans came to be drawn directly on the mount in black ink and color-painted, instead of being pasted on.

A example of a hari-ezu, a plan drawn on a separate paper, cut out and pasted on the mount. (Ceremonial hall for the Daizyosai, built in the south courtyard of the Sisiden.)

貼絵図の例（紫震殿の南庭に作られた大嘗祭の式場）

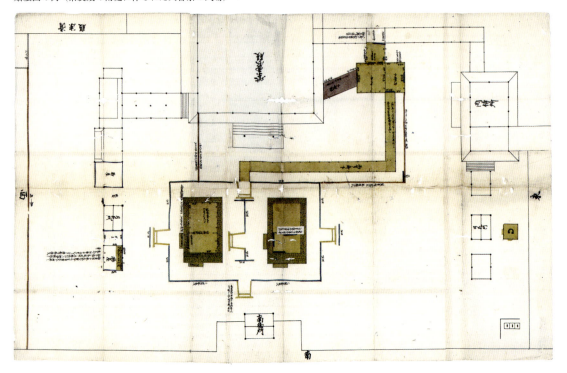

47 建築工事－2　建築図面－1

　江戸時代にも、建物を建てるとき、様々な図面が作られました。基本は、全体を把握するために敷地全体に建物の平面を配置した指図です。指図の縮尺は、一間を二分に縮めた「二分計」、六分の「六分計」、一寸の「一寸計」が一般的で、場合によって四分、八分なども使われました。現在の言い方に直すと、一寸計は1間（6尺5寸）が1寸となりますから、65分の1の縮尺。六分計は約108分の1ということです。

　貼絵図　製作順序は、先ず敷地の大きさが入る台紙を白い紙で作り、半間間隔の格子を箆で引きます。個々の建物の平面図は別紙で作り、切りとって台紙に貼っていきます。西暦1700年頃からは、格子を墨線あるいは朱線で引くものも見られるようになります。建物の平面図は、江戸時代初めの慶長頃は白、元和頃からは花色、寛永になると花色の建物の周りの縁側を柿色で示すようになり、明暦頃から屋根材、床の別などで色分けするようになります。

　書絵図　1700年頃からは、平面を別紙で貼るのではなく、台紙に直接平面を墨線で描き、色を塗るようになります。

An example of a *kaki-ezu*, a plan drawn directly on the mount. Part of the *sasizu* of the residence of the main enclosure, Edo Castle, （built in the first year of the Man'en era）.

書絵図の例　江戸城本丸御殿（万延度）指図の部分

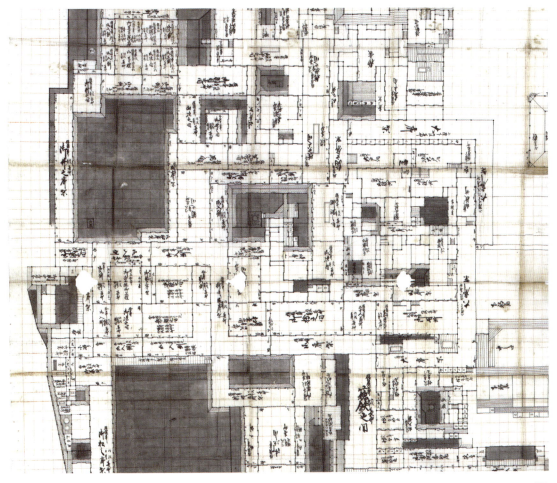

48 Building Construction Work 3. Architectural Drawings 2.

Besides the procedures to be followed for the *sasizu*, which showed the construction work in its entirety, the shogunate prescribed "Ways to Prepare Drawings for Construction."

For important buildings such as the Ōhiroma, Sirosyoin and Gozanoma, a three-dimensional model (*okosiezu*) at 1:32.5 scale was made to obtain opinions on the design. After the design was decided, drawings that had received seals of approval from four officials in charge of respectively finances (*kanzyō-kata*), construction (*sakuzi-kata*), surveillance (*metuke-kata*) and investigation (*gimmi-kata*) were passed on to lower officials.

Conventional plans were submitted for other reception rooms, and once a design was decided, different types of drawings were prepared for each aspect of construction work.

An example of a *zi-ezu*, a plan with posts indicated by a seal, and doors and finish are drawn in detail. The main reception hall of the residence of the main enclosure, Edo Castle（built in the first year of the Man'en era）. "Gohonmaru Ōhiroma ziezu." (Central Library, Tokyo Metropolitan Library)

地絵図の例　江戸城本丸御殿大広間（万延度）『御本丸大広間地絵図』（都立中央図書館特別文庫室蔵）

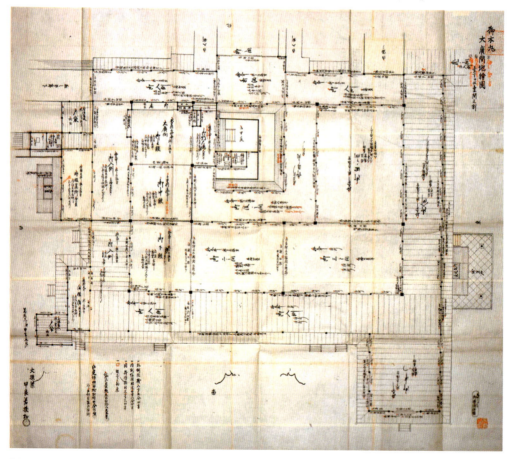

48 建築工事-3 建築図面-2

　全体を描いた指図以外は、幕府は『御普請絵図類仕立方』として、規定しています。
　大広間、白書院、御座之間等主要な建物は1間を2寸の縮尺で作った立体的な起絵図で意向を伺い、決定のうえ、勘定方、作事方、目付方、吟味方が調印した物が下げ渡されます。
　その外の座敷は従来通りの平面図を伺いに差し出し、決定したら、区分ごとに、次の種類の図面を作ったのです。

地絵図　一寸計。平面図に柱を印で押し、戸や造作を明細に書き込む。
地形絵図　一寸計。地絵図同様に作り、荷持柱を区別して印で押し、柱間寸法を書き込む
土台絵図　一寸計。土台を色分けし、柱間寸法を書き込む。
足堅め大引絵図　一寸計。足堅めは黄色、大引は二筋の朱線、束は朱の星印、柱間寸法を書き込む。
二階梁配絵図　一寸計。二階梁などを色分けし、柱、下管柱は黒四角、上管柱は朱星。
小屋梁配絵図　一寸計。敷梁、小屋梁などを色分けし、軒先、谷、棟、母屋などを朱線で示し、梁の割り付けなどは寸法を書き込む。
屋根水取絵図　一寸計。平面を墨線で、屋根伏せを朱線で描き、軒高を明細に書き込む。
天井絵図　三〇分の一。格縁、猿頬、棹縁の寸法を明細に書き込む。
建地割絵図　二〇分の一。妻、平側の小屋組み、内部造作などまで図に示し、明細に寸法を書き込む。
軒矩計絵図　一〇分の一。礎石から軒まで、桁高、軒出、床高、内法高等明細に寸法を書き込む。
正寸絵図　長押、鴨居、敷居、帳台構、棚廻りなどを描き、詳細に寸法を書き込む。
御床御棚廻り　一〇分の一．明細に。
絵様類正寸　懸魚、鬼瓦、蟇股などを明細に。

　その上、絵図は美濃紙を継ぎ合わせて作ること、写しを三通つくって、大棟梁の控一通、上場所、下拵所にそれぞれ一通づつ回し、肝煎りの持ち場の絵図は大棟梁の検印を受けること、と定めています。

Two examples of a *tateziwari-ezu*. (Central Library, Tokyo Metropolitan Library)

江戸城大広間の建地割
上：南北断面図、『御本丸大広間南御入側より御上段後御入側二十分の一総建地割』
下：南正面図、『御本丸大広間南面建地割』
（五十分ノ一）
（都立中央図書館特別文庫室蔵）

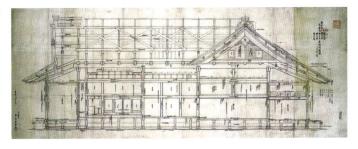

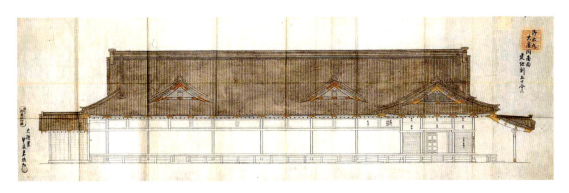

49 Building Construction Work 4 Post-and-Beam (Frame) Construction

Traditional Japanese architecture is of wooden construction and has post-and-beam structures.

The lower ends of posts in post-and-beam construction were originally planted directly in the ground. Later they were erected on stone bases, and still later on sills. Beams were assembled on the top of those posts. Struts erected on the top of beams supported purlins and the ridge pole, completing the basic framing for the roof. Then the roofing was laid, the flooring assembled, the upper and lower runners and sliding panels installed and the walls constructed, completing the building.

"Gohonmaru Ōhiroma asigatame-ezu."（Central Library, Tokyo Metropolitan Library）The drawing shows the stone base and sleepers.
『御本丸大広間足堅絵図』（都立中央図書館特別文庫室蔵）土台および大引きを示す図

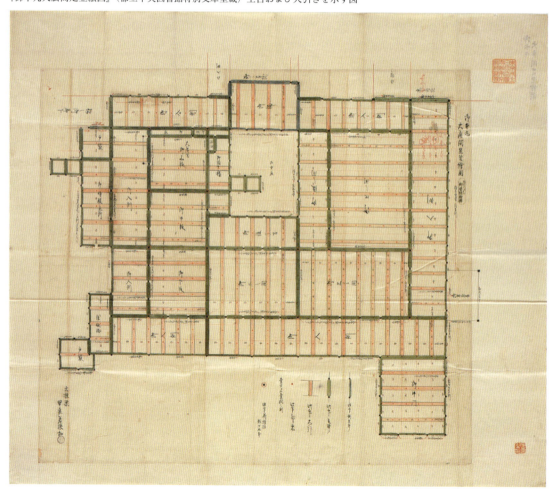

49　建築工事－4　軸組構法

　日本の建築は木造で、柱梁等で構成される軸組構法です。

　軸組は、掘立から、礎石の上に柱を立てるようになり、さらに、土台を設けるように変化しますが、その柱の上に桁や梁を組みます。梁の上に立てた束柱に母屋、棟木を置いて屋根の下地ができます。屋根を葺き、床を組み、開口部には敷居・鴨居に建具を立て、壁を作って、建物が出来上がります。

　日本の近世建築は、基本的に軸組構法です。

These drawings in the possession of the Central Library, Tokyo Metropolitan Library, were related to construction work on the Residence of the Main Enclosure, Edo Castle, in the first year of the Man'en era.
いずれも都立中央図書館特別文庫室蔵の万延度江戸城本丸御殿作事にかかわる絵図。

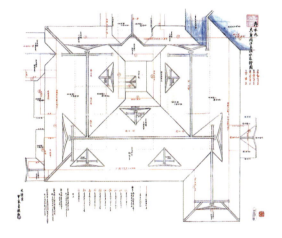

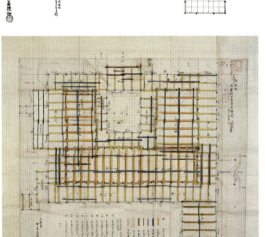

Above left: "Gohonmaru Ōhiroma gōtenzyō-ezu" (Drawing of the Coffered Ceiling of the Large Reception Hall in the Main Enclosure).
Below left: "Gohonmaru Ōhiroma koyabarikubari-ezu" (Drawing of the Arrangement of Tie Beams of the Large Reception Hall in the Main Enclosure).
Above right: "Gohonmaru Ohiroma oyane-mizutori-ezu" (Drawing of the Roof Slopes of the Large Reception Hall in the Main Enclosure)

左上：『御本丸大広間格天井絵図』
左下：『御本丸大広間小屋梁配絵図』
右上：『御本丸大広間御屋根水取絵図』

50 Building Construction Work 5 Walls

Different types of walls included the *itakabe* (wall covered with wood boards), *haritukekabe* (papered panel installed in a frame), and *tutikabe* (clay wall). There were also stone walls, but these were for special uses.

Walls can be classified roughly into two categories, depending on the treatment of structural posts: the *ōkabe* in which posts were concealed, and the *sinkabe* in which the posts were revealed. The *sinkabe* was widely used.

Houses generally had wattle-and-daub walls in which posts were revealed, but *haritukekabe* with paintings drawn on them were used in upper-class houses. Gold foil was sometime used on the background for *haritukekabe* with paintings. The posts could be concealed in *itakabe* used as an exterior wall.

Clay walls with concealed posts were used in castle structures such as donjons and towers and in storehouses to provide protection from fire.

Penetrating ties (*nuki*) formed the underpinning for a wall. These horizontal members passed through posts at several levels. In a *haritukekabe*, a panel was installed over these ties and its edges secured to posts by means of so-called *sibuiti* (wooden sticks that were 7.5mm x 7.5mm in cross section and painted in black lacquer). In a clay wall, split bamboo members, arranged vertically and horizontally and tied together with rope were added to the penetrating ties to form the basic substructure which was called the *komai*. Soil was daubed on the *komai* and pressed from both sides to form the undercoat. Clayey soil from the beds of rice paddies was used. The soil was kneaded together with straw. When the undercoat had dried, the middle coat was applied. Where the posts were to be concealed, ropes attached to the surface of the undercoat were incorporated into the second coat to prevent the second coat from separating. Time was taken in the middle-coat stage to make certain the clay was completely dry. Then came the final coat. In a white wall, hemp fibers were mixed with white clay to prevent cracks. From the middle of the Edo period, plaster came to be used for white walls. Plaster was kneaded with paste, produced by boiling seaweed, before being applied. A colored wall was finished with plaster mixed with either colored clay or a pigment such as red ocher. White walls were the norm in castle buildings, but red walls (walls colored red produced by adding red ocher pigment to the plaster) were occasionally used, for example in Kumamoto Castle, in some parts of a type of wall called *tuizibei*, the exterior wall of an inner room in the residence of the main enclosure and the storehouse.

"Isyokuzyū no uti kasyoku osanaetoki no zu," (drawings intended to teach children about trades having to do with clothing, food and shelter). Bamboo is split for the wall substructure. (Wood shingles are used for the roofing.)

『衣食住之内家職幼絵解之図』
壁の小舞竹をかく。(屋根では杮（こけら）を葺いている)

50　建築工事−5　壁

　壁には、板を貼った板壁、フレームに紙を貼ったパネルをはめた貼付壁、土を塗った土壁があります。石積の壁もありますが、日本では特殊です。

　壁の構造体の柱などとの取り合いによって、柱を見せない大壁、柱を見せる真壁に分類できます。真壁が、広く使われています。

　住宅は、土壁の真壁が普通ですが、上層階級の住宅では、表面に絵を描いた張付壁が使われています。絵を描いた張付壁には、地に金箔を貼ることもあります。外壁の板壁には大壁の場合があります。

　土壁の大壁は、天守や櫓などの城郭建築や、土蔵などで、外からの火災を防ぐために使われます。

　壁の下地の基本は、柱に通した貫です。貫は水平に数段設けます。張付壁は、その上にパネルをはめ、周囲を四分一（一辺 7.5㎜ [4分の1寸]の方形断面の黒漆塗りの木の棒）で柱に止めます。土壁の下地は、貫を基本に、縦横に割竹を縄で組んで作ります。これを小舞といいます。

　小舞に土をつけ、両側から押さえて下塗りとします。この土には、田の底の粘土質の土が使われました。土には藁苆が練り込まれます。下塗りが乾くと、中塗りになります。大壁の場合、下塗りの面に下げた縄を中塗りに塗りこめて、中塗りが剥離するのを防ぎます。中塗りの段階で、完全に乾かすために時間をかけます。

　最後は、上塗りです。白い壁は、白土に麻の繊維を苆として混ぜ、ひび割れを防ぎます。江戸時代の中ごろからは、白い壁に漆喰が使われるようになります。漆喰は、布海苔を煮た糊でこねて使います。色壁は、色土か弁柄などの顔料によって色を付けた漆喰で仕上げます。城郭建築は白壁が普通ですが、熊本城のように、築地塀の一部や、住まいである本丸御殿の奥の部屋の外壁、土蔵に赤壁（漆喰に顔料として弁柄を加えた赤色の壁）が使われた場合がありました。

Left：Applying the undercoat for a wall. Straw is being cut below.　　*Right*：Applying the final coat for a wall.

左：壁の下塗り。下では苆（すさ）を切っている。　　　　　　　　　　右：壁の上塗り

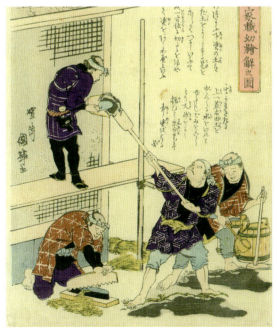

51 Building Construction Work 6 Roofing

Clay tiles were ordinarily used. Clay shaped in a tile mold is dried and fired in a kiln. When the mouth of the kiln is closed at the end of the firing process and the clay is baked, the surface of the tile, covered with fine particles of carbon soot, becomes silver in color. This silver-colored tile weathers with time and blackens. Tile inevitably absorbs water because the firing temperature is low. Clay tile is not suited to cold regions because the freezing of its water content may produce exfoliation or even cracks, which leads to leaks. To counter this, metal shingles, stone tiles and red tiles were used.

There were also wood shingles, though they were not suitable for all castle structures. Copper, lead and white wax were some of the materials used in metal sheets. Though a castle structure may be described as roofed in copper tiles or lead tiles, these are not genuine tiles; instead, a backing resembling a genuine roof tile was made from wood and covered with a metal sheet.

Copper roof tiles are to be found on the donjons of Nagoya and Hirosaki Castles. Lead roof tiles are distinctive to Kanazawa Castle. White wax was used on the donjon of Sumpu Castle built by Tokugawa Ieyasu.

Syakudaniisi, a tuffaceous stone from the Etizen region, was used for stone tiles found in Hukui and Maruoka Castles.

The towers in Hirosaki Castle were roofed in wood boards. However, since these were not durable, the boards were covered with copper.

Red tiles (*akagawara*) were created in Etizen sometime after the middle of the Edo period. These tiles were dipped in water mixed with red ocher before firing. The red ocher melted and became a glaze, making the tiles impervious to water. As a result, red tiles came to be widely used in cold regions. They can be found on the Sea of Japan side of Honsyu from Hukui Prefecture northward, and in western Hokkaido from Hakodate to about Otaru.

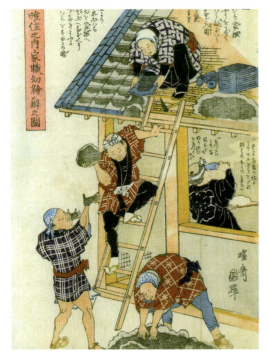

"Isyokuzyū no uti kasyoku osanaetoki no zu." *Kawarabuki* roof
『衣食住之内家職幼絵解之図』瓦葺

51 建築工事－6　屋根を葺く

　普通に使われるのは、土瓦です。土瓦は、粘土を瓦の型にあてて成形してから乾燥し、窯に入れて焼きます。焼成の最後に口を閉めて蒸し焼きにすると、煤の炭素の微粒子が表面について銀色になります。この銀色の瓦は、年月が経つと風化して炭素の黒い色になるのです。焼成温度が高くないのでどうしても水気を吸い、寒い地域では寒気で水分が凍って、表面がはがれるように割れたり、最悪ひびが入ってしまいます。漏るようになるので、土瓦は寒冷地には向きません。

　そこで工夫されたのが、金属板や、石瓦、赤瓦です。場合によっては、城にはむいていないのですが、板葺ということもありました。

　金属板には、銅、鉛、白鑞などが使われました。銅瓦葺・鉛瓦葺と呼ばれていますが、実際には木で本瓦に似た形の下地を作り、その上に金属板を張りました。銅瓦は、名古屋城天守、弘前城天守で見ることができます。鉛瓦葺は、金沢城の特色です。白鑞は、徳川家康が造った駿府城の天守に使われていました。

　石瓦は、越前の笏谷石が使われ、福井城・丸岡城で見られます。弘前城の櫓は板葺でしたが、耐久性がないので、現在は、形はそのままに、その上に銅板をかけています。

　赤瓦は、江戸時代の半ば過ぎに越前で作られるようになった瓦で、弁柄を混ぜた水に漬けて表面に弁柄をかけてから焼いています。弁柄が溶けて釉薬になり、水分を吸わなくなるので、寒い地域に広まりました。福井県から北の日本海側から、北海道の西側の函館から小樽くらいの地域で見ることができます。

Above left：Stone（Shakudaniisi）. *Bellow left*：lead tile roof. *Above right*：shingle（board）roof. *Bellow right*：akagawara file roof.

左上、石瓦葺（笏谷石）。左下、鉛瓦葺。右上、板葺。右下、赤瓦葺。

52 Building Construction Work 7 Ridge (*Ōmune*, *Kudarimune*, *Sumimune*), *Onigawara*, *Syati*

A ridge is built where two roof surfaces meet. For example, on the highest roof of a donjon, the horizontal "main ridge" (*ōmune*) is at the top; "descending ridges" (*kudarimune*) extend downward from the ends of the main ridge, following the surface of the roof, and "corner ridges" (*sumimune*) start where the descending ridges end and extend to the outer corners of the roof.

A ridge is created by stacking roof tiles, and semi-cylindrically-shaped roof tiles are placed on the very top. Special tiles called "ogre tiles" (*onigawara*) are used to cover the ends of a ridge so that the stacking of the tiles is not revealed in cross section.

Ogre tiles are so called because the face of a demon is sculpted on their surface, but in the case of a castle, the family crest of the lord of the castle was often used instead. *Toribusuma*, an extension of the semicylindrical tiles on the top of the ridge, was installed above the ogre tile. At both ends of the main ridge at the very top of a donjon were large tiles in the shape of imaginary marine creatures called *syati*. Smaller *syati* were sometimes also arranged on the ridges of dormer gables (*tidorihahu*) and undulating gables (*karahahu*) on lower levels. The two *syati* on the main ridge were designed as a pair.

Above left: the eaves of a *hongawara* roof, *Above right*: the eaves of lead tile roof, *Below*: *hongawara* being laid.
上左：本瓦葺の軒先　上右：鉛瓦葺の軒先　下：本瓦を葺いているところ

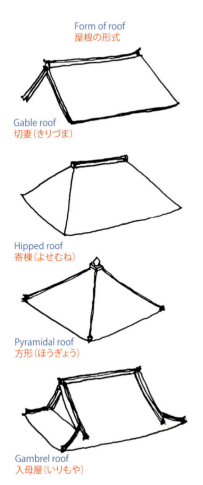

Form of roof
屋根の形式

Gable roof
切妻（きりづま）

Hipped roof
寄棟（よせむね）

Pyramidal roof
方形（ほうぎょう）

Gambrel roof
入母屋（いりもや）

52 建築工事-7 棟（大棟・下り棟・隅棟）、鬼瓦・鯱

　屋根は、各面の合わさるところに、棟を作ります。例えば、天守の一番上の屋根では、頂部にあるのが大棟、大棟の端から屋根面に沿って下っているのが下り棟、下り棟の終わりころから屋根の四方の外角に向かうのが隅棟です。棟は、瓦を積んで作り、一番上に半円筒形の瓦を伏せます。

　棟の両端は、そのままでは瓦を積んだ断面が見えてしまうので、特別な瓦で断面をふさぎます。その瓦が、鬼瓦です。表に鬼の顔を彫刻するので、鬼瓦といいますが、城ではしばしば城主の家紋をつけます。

　鬼瓦の上に、棟の一番上の丸瓦をのばした鳥衾をつけます。天守の一番上の大棟の両端には、鯱（想像上の海獣）の形をした大きな瓦を上げます。下の階の千鳥破風や唐破風の棟にも、小さな鯱をつけることがあります。大棟の一対の鯱は、阿吽にします。

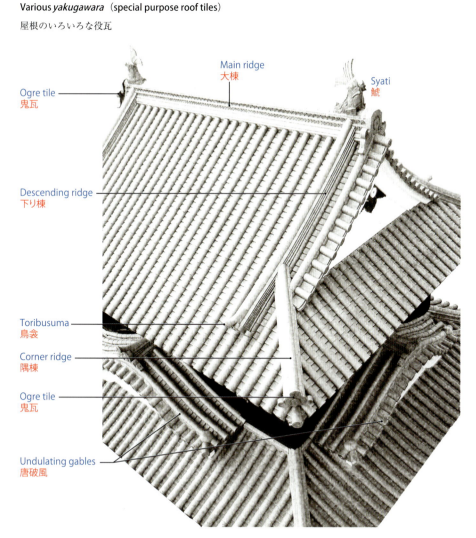

Various *yakugawara* (special purpose roof tiles)
屋根のいろいろな役瓦

53 Building Construction Work 8 Ceremonies of Carpenters

Of the ceremonies observed in connection with building construction work, the representative ones are the *zitinsai*, held at the outset in which prayers are offered to the spirits (*kami*) of the land, and the *zyōtōsai*, celebrated upon completion in a place of ceremony prepared on top of the roof. In between these ceremonies, events are held such as the *tyōna-hazime*, where a line is inked on a piece of lumber and the first cut is made with an adze; the *kuwa-hazime*, where ground is broken for the first time with a hoe; and the *rittyu*, where the first post is erected. Of all these ceremonies, the most splendid is the *zyōtōsai*.

The *zyōtōsai*, held when the building has taken shape and the structure has been assembled, celebrates the raising of the ridge beam to the top of the roof and its installation upon struts. Prayers for safety are offered. In a full-fledged work of building construction in the Edo period, a deck was constructed on top of the completed roof, three *gohei* (strips of paper used in Sinto rituals) were hung and bows fixed with arrows pointing toward heaven and earth were positioned atop the ridge, and an altar with offerings was prepared on the deck. Then ropes were hung from the ridge, and the participants would make gestures simulating the pulling up of the ridge beam by the ropes and its installation on the struts, to shouts of encouragement from the master carpenter. A ceremony would be held inside the building as well, including the performance of *kagura* (sacred music and dancing). At its end, the ceremonial stowing of the adze (*tyōna-osame*), signifying the end of construction work, was performed, and rice cakes were scattered from a tower to the people gathered there. A Buddhist ceremony of prayer for peace and tranquility was performed, and the new building was ready for use.

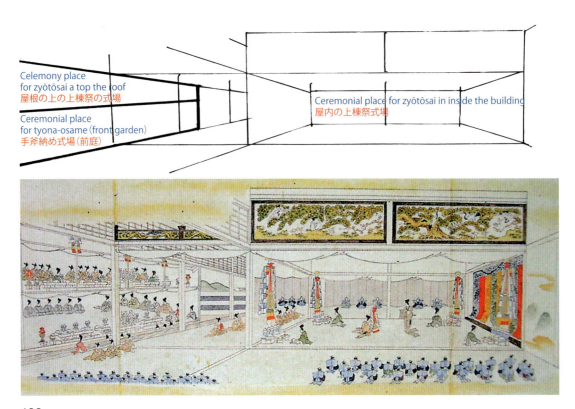

53 建築工事-8 大工の儀式

　作事（建築工事）に際して行われる儀式は、開始に際して地の神を祭る地鎮祭にはじまり、完成して屋根の上に祭場を作って祝う上棟祭が代表的なもので、その間に、材木に墨を打ち、手斧で其の材木を初めて削る手斧始、最初に土に鍬を入れる鍬始、最初の柱を建てる立柱、などが行われます。その中で最も華やかなのが、上棟祭です。

　上棟祭は、本来の意味は、建築の形が見えるようになる、構造が組みあがり、屋根の一番上に乗る棟木を引き上げ、棟束の上に据えることを祝い、無事を祈るのですが、江戸時代の本格的な作事では、完成した屋根の上にデッキを作り、棟の上に御幣3本と天と地に向かう矢をつがえた弓を立て、デッキの上に御供えをした祭壇をつくります。

　そして、棟から綱を下におろして、参列した人々が綱を引いて棟木を引き上げ、棟木を束に打ち据えるゼスチュアが、棟梁の掛け声によって進行します。室内でも榊を立て玉女が神楽を舞うなどして、儀式が行われます。終わると、工事が終わったことを意味する手斧納めが行われ、集まった人々に櫓から餅が撒かれました。その上に仏式の安鎮が修法されたうえ、新しい建物が使われ始めるのです。

Jōtōsai, "Daiku zyōtō no zu"

上棟祭『大工上棟之図』（國貞）

下：餅撒き『辰年御規式之図』

Below, the scattering of rice cakes. The open space from outside Nisihane Bridge to outside the Kitazume guardhouse, "Tatudosi Onkisiki nozu"

Opposite page：
The *zyōtōsai* and the ceremonial stowing away of the adze at the Ōoku reception hall（*taimenzyo*）, Edo Castle.

左頁：
江戸城大奥対面所での上棟祭と手斧納め
『辰年御規式之図』

54 Building Construction Work 9 Carpenter's Tools

for cutting down a tree: *ono* (ax); ①
for measuring : *kanezyaku* (steel square), *kenzao* (a wood pole, one *ken* in length); ②
for drawing lines, marking: *sumitsubo* (ink pot), *sumisashi* (bamboo ink marker); ③
for making rough cuts: *ono* (ax); ①
for cutting: *nokogiri* (saw); ④ *oga* (frame saw); ⑤ *daigiri* (pit saw); *maebiki* (rip saw) ⑥
for whittling and shaving: *tyōna* (adze) ⑦, *yariganna* (planing knife), *kanna* (plane) ⑧, small knives (*kogatana*, *kiridashi*);
for striking: *kanazuti* (hammer for nails and clamps), *kakeya* (large wooden mallet for piles and beams), *saizuti* (small wooden hammer for planes and chisels), *gennō* ⑨ (steel double-faced hammer for Chisel);
for extracting nails: *kugi-nuki* (nail extractor);
for making a hole: *kiri* (gimlet), *maigiri* (bow drill), *moziri* (spiral drill), *namban-moziri* (bolt drill); ⑩
for digging a hole: *nomi* (chisel); ⑪
for repair and maintenance: *toisi* (whetstone) ⑫, *metate-dōgu* (tools for sharpening the teeth and adjusting the set of saws).

ono tyōna maebiki oga (in the collection of the Takenaka Carpentry Tools Museum)
斧 手斧 前挽 大鋸（竹中大工道具館蔵）

① Ono (ax) 斧
⑦ Tyōna (adze) 手斧
⑥ Maebiki (ripsaw) 前挽
⑤ Oga (frame saw) 大鋸

54 建築工事－9　大工道具

樹を伐る　斧①

測る　曲尺②　間棹

線を引く・印をつける　墨壺・墨差し③

材を切りだす　斧①

材を切る　鋸④　大鋸⑤　台切　前挽⑥

削る　手斧⑦　鑓鉋　鉋⑧

打つ　（釘を・鏨を）金槌　（杭を・梁を）掛矢　（鉋を・鑿を）才槌　（鑿を）玄能⑨

釘を抜く　釘抜き

穴をあける　四ッ目錐⑩（三ッ目錐）　舞錐　南蛮捻り

穴をほる　鑿⑪

修理・保全道具　砥石⑫・目立て道具

釘　鎹

sumitubo sumisasi kanna toisi kanezyaku tukinomi tatakinomi nokogiri saizuti kiri (in the collection of the Takenaka Carpentry Tools Museum)

黒壺　黒差し　鉋　砥石　曲尺　突き鑿　叩き鑿　鋸　玄能　（竹中大工道具館蔵　錐を除く）

③ Sumitubo (ink pot)
墨壺

③ Bamboo brush for marking
墨差し

⑧ Kanna (plane)
鉋

⑨ Genno (hammer)
玄能

④ Nokogiri (saw)
鋸

⑩ kiri (gimlet)
錐

② Kanezyaku (steel square)
曲尺

⑪ Stab chisel
突き鑿

⑪ Chisel for hand-tooled finish
叩き鑿

⑫ Toisi (whetstone)
砥石

109

55 Residence in the Castle and Residences of Retainers outside the Castle-1 (Syoin-zukuri)

Retainers outside the castle Retainers from those who were most senior (*karō*) to lowly foot soldiers (*asigaru*) lived in residences supplied by the domain (*han*). There were standards set for the size of the site and the size and layout of the residence, depending on the retainer's stipend. The standards for one domain could differ from those of another, depending on the size of the domain. Similar conditions prevailed in Edo, the castle-town of the shogunate.

Daimyō Residences in Edo and Residences of Castle Lords *Samurai* residences in the Edo period for example, daimyo residences in Edo and the residence of the lord of a castle, were in the style known as *syoin-zukuri*. The style was established shortly after the start of the Edo period in the Genna and Kan'ei eras (1615-44).

Residences in the *syoin* style were organized around a hall called the *syoin* where the master of the house, for example a *daimyō*, had audiences with his retainers. (In the case of a *samurai* of high rank, there were both a large *syoin* and a small *syoin*.) In the front part of the *syoin* was the "large room" (*hiroma*) to which was attached an entrance hall facing the main gate (*omote-mon*). In the back of these were the *ima-syoin* where everyday affairs of state were administered and the hall (*goten*) where the master of the house lived. Behind these were such rooms as the staff room (*tumesyo*) where retainers worked, and the kitchen. All the above were collectively referred to as the *omote*, that is, the front, official area. Behind the *omote*, was a compound for private life called the *oku*, that is, the inner area.

A *syoin* consisted of a suite of two to three rooms arranged in a row, with the innermost room with a slightly elevated floor referred to as the *zyōdan-no-ma*. At the far end of the *zyōdan-no-ma* were a *tokonoma* alcove and staggered shelves (*tigaidana*). Sharing a corner post with the *tokonoma* was a built-in desk (*tuke-syoin*) on the side of the room facing a garden, and sharing a corner post with the staggered shelves and across the room from the built-in desk was a set of decorative doors (*tyōdaigamae*).

Interior design of the *syoin*, around which residences in the *syoin* style were organized.　書院造を構成する書院の室内意匠

55 城内の御殿・城下の藩士の屋敷－1（書院造）

城下の藩士の屋敷　藩士たちは、家老から足軽に至るまで、藩から支給された屋敷に住んでいました。支給される屋敷には、藩士の禄高によって、敷地の面積、住居の規模や平面に基準がありました。その基準は、藩の大小によって異なりました。このような状況は、幕府の城下町である江戸においても同様でした。

大名の屋敷　江戸時代の武家屋敷の様式は、書院造です。大名の江戸屋敷や城内の御殿はその典型です。書院造が成立したのは、江戸時代に入って間もない元和・寛永時代です。

書院造は、大名などの主人が家臣と対面する、書院と呼ばれる御殿（上級の武士の場合には大書院と小書院）を中心に構成され、その表に、表門に面して玄関が附属する広間が、書院の背後に、日常の政務のための居間書院や起居のための御殿が配置され、これらの背後に、家臣等が勤務する詰所や台所などがありました。これらの部分全体を「表（おもて）」と呼んでいました。表のさらに奥に、「奥」と呼ばれた私生活のための一郭がありました。

書院は、一列に2～3室を並べ、奥の部屋の床（ゆか）を一段上げた上段の間とします。上段の間には、奥の面に床と違棚、床の隅の柱を共用して庭に面する側に付書院、違棚の隅の柱を共用して付書院に面して帳台構を設けます。

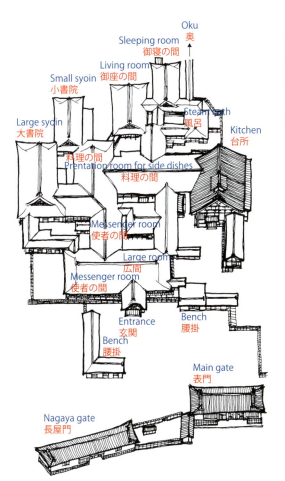

Right, the main residence (*kamiyasiki*) of a domain located outside Hibiya Gate.
Left, bird eye view the *omote* (official area) of the second residence (*nakayasiki*) of the Uwazima Domain, located in the Azabu district of Edo.

右：日比谷門外の長州藩江戸上屋敷
左：宇和島藩麻布江戸中屋敷表の鳥瞰図

56 Residence in the Castle and Residences of Retainers outside the Castle-2 (Before the Development of the Shoin Style)

Hommaru Palace in Edo Castle; Ninomaru Palace in Nizyō Castle

In the Ninomaru Palace in Nizyō Castle, built in the early Edo period, the main halls were called Ōhiroma and Kohiroma. Moreover, in the Hommaru Palace in Edo Castle, which was the office of the Tokugawa shogunate, the Ōhiroma continued to be built throughout the Edo period. Until the formation of the *syoin* style, residences that retained a protruding entrance corridor (*tyūmon*), a vestige of the earlier *syuden* style, were built. The Ninomaru Palace of Nizyō Castle does not have an entrance corridor attached to it, but like the Ōhiroma in the Hommaru Palace in Edo Castle, it does have a complex plan. The complex plan too is a vestige of the medieval *shuden* style, in which one central building contained both places for ceremonies and functions and places for everyday life.

In the Hommaru Palace of Edo Castle, the buildings adjoining the Ōhiroma came to be called the Sirosyoin and Kurosyoin. These subsequently built places for rest and small audiences had *syoin*-style layouts of rooms arranged in a row. Similarly, in the Ninomaru Palace of Nizyo Castle, which was not used from the Kan'ei era until the end of the shogunate, the Kohiroma came to be called the Kurosyoin.

Daimyō residences in Edo in the early Edo period were still under the influence of the *syuden* style, but after the Great Meireki Fire of 1657, many of them were rebuilt in the *syoin* style.

Residence and garden of Ninomaru Residence, Nizyō Castle. (The parts drawn in single line no longer exist.)

二条城二の丸御殿の御殿と庭園（シングルラインの平面は現在はない）

56　城内の御殿・城下の藩士の屋敷－2（書院造が出来るまで）

　江戸城の本丸御殿・二条城二の丸御殿　　江戸時代初期に造られた二条城二の丸御殿では、中心となる御殿を、大広間、小広間と呼んでいました。また、江戸時代を通じて江戸幕府の政庁であった江戸城本丸御殿では、大広間を造り続けました。ほかにも書院造が成立するまで、中門を表側に突出する主殿形式の名残を残す御殿が建てられました。二条城の二の丸御殿は、中門は付属していませんが、江戸城本丸御殿大広間と同様に、複雑な平面をしています。この複雑な平面も、1つの中心となる建物が、儀式、行事の場と生活の場を含んだ中世の主殿形式の名残です。

　江戸城本丸御殿では、大広間に続く御殿を白書院・黒書院と呼ぶようになります。後から新設された御休息や御小座敷は一列型の書院造の平面になっています。また、寛永以来幕末まで使われることがなかった二条城の二の丸御殿でも、小広間を黒書院と呼ぶように変わっています。

　江戸における大名の江戸屋敷でも、江戸時代の初期には主殿形式の影響が残っていましたが、明暦江戸大火後に多くは書院造で再築されました。

Plan of the *omote*（official area）and *nakaoku*（the syōgun's private quarters）of the residence of the main enclosure, Edo Castle, built in the first year of the Man'en era.
"Edozyō Gohonmaru Man'endo gohusin gotenmuki omoteoku sōezu"（in the possession of the Central Library, Tokyo Metropolitan Library）.
万延度江戸城本丸御殿表、中奥平面図
『江戸城御本丸万延度御普請御殿向表奥惣絵図』（都立中央図書館特別文庫室蔵）

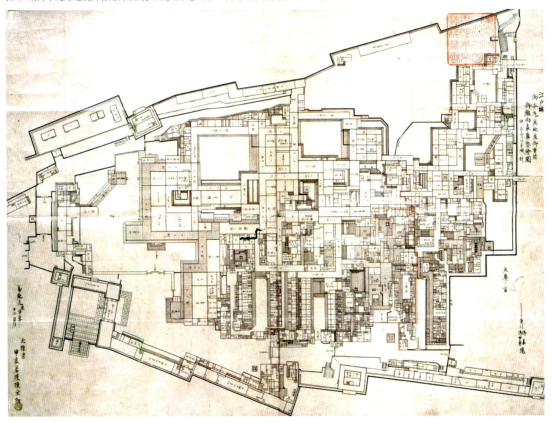

57 Residence in the Castle and Residences of Retainers outside the Castle 3. Residences of Retainers outside the Castle

It is not known whether there were standards for every castle town, but some domains clearly had standard plans and rules concerning the presence or absence of ceilings and specifications for walls, depending on the rank of the retainer.

In the Ueda domain, for which historical material survives, plans were indicated for seven different grades of residence, from a house for the most senior retainer (*karō*) to a rowhouse for a foot soldier (*asigaru*), and appended notes specified if a room was to have a ceiling or not or where red walls were to be installed. In the plan of the highest grade, there was an entrance hall with a boarded area (*sikidai*) in front, and the front, formal portion of the house was organized around a *syoin* and an anteroom. The kitchen and the rooms for family life were arranged in the back. The *syoin* possessed a *tokonoma* alcove, staggered shelves, battened ceilings (*saobuti tenzyō*) and red ocher walls. There are extant *samurai* residences in Ueda (Nagano Prefecture) that are believed to have been built in accord with set standards.

A *samurai* residence of this kind was laid out so that its front, formal portion was on the side closer to the street on which the gate opened. It is the convention in contemporary Japanese houses to orient the living room in a southern direction for greater exposure to the sun, but arranging the layout of buildings with a southern exposure in mind is believed to have begun from the latter half to the end of the eighteenth century at the earliest.

Standard plans for samurai residences of the Ueda domain (in what is now Nagano Prefecture). grade 1 : 94 *tubo* [1 *tubo* = approximately 3.3 square meters]

上田藩（長野県）の武家屋敷の基準となる平面（定法）

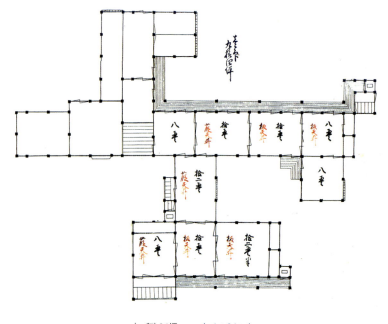

〈一印〉94坪　grade 1 : 94 *tubo*

57　城内の御殿・城下の藩士の屋敷－3　城下の家臣たちの住まい

　それぞれの城下町に基準があったかはわかっていませんが、一部の藩では、藩士の階層に合わせて、基準の平面図やこれに伴う天井の有無や壁の仕様が示されていました。

　史料が残っている上田の例では、家老クラスの最上層から、足軽クラスの長屋まで、7階層の平面図が示され、天井の有無や赤壁とする箇所が付記されています。最上層の平面（114頁）を見ると、敷台玄関を備え、次の間をもつ一列型の書院が表の中心で、奥に台所や家族が生活する部屋を設けています。書院には、床の間、違棚があり、天井は棹縁天井、赤壁です。上田では、現存する武家屋敷に、標準によっていると思われる例がみられます。

　このような武家屋敷は、いずれも門を開く道路側を表として、建物が配置されています。現代の日本の住宅では、陽がよく当たるように居間などを南に面するよう配置するのが常識ですが、南を意識して建物が配置され始めるのは、早い地域でも18世紀後半から末と考えられます。

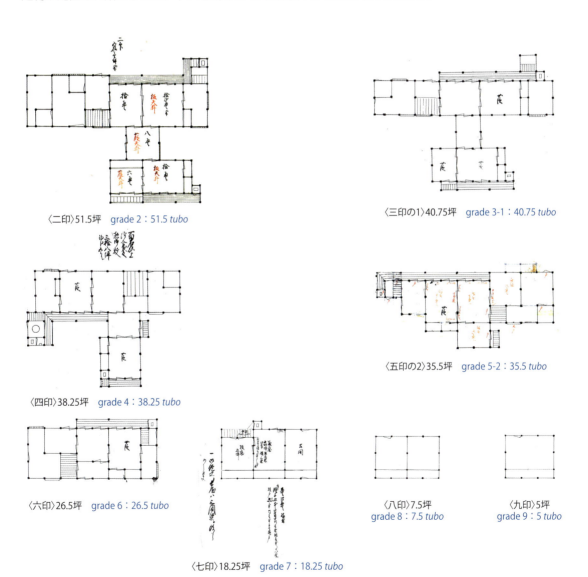

58 Residence in the Castle and Residences of Retainers outside the Castle 4. Daimyō Estates Dedicated to Pastimes and Buildings for Relaxation

Castle residences of *daimyō* in their respective domains and their main residences (*kami-yasiki*) in Edo were all in the *syoin* style. Other than the paintings on sliding doors and screens, there was not much difference in the way those residences were built from one domain to the next.

It was in the villas (*simo-yasiki*) built in Edo and outside the castles in their domains that *daimyō* demonstrated their culture and taste. Kōrakuen and Rikugien in Edo, Kōrakuen in Okayama, Riturin Garden in Takamatu, Suizenzi Park in Kumamoto, and Kenrokuen in Kanazawa are among the villas still extant. Katsura Detached Palace in Kyoto was also a villa, but it was for the Hatizyō-no-miya family who were members of the court nobility rather than the samurai class. The lord of Himezi Castle built the so-called opposite estate (*mukai-yasiki*) with a large pond, a hillock, and structures such as a *sukiya* (tea house) and bath house within the inner enclosures.

The opposite estate was organized around the Umbrella Room (Karakasa-no-ma(cf. p23)), measuring eight *ken* square and equipped with a long hearth, and steps led down to the pond from a veranda on the north side of the building. From there a boat took one to a tea house on top of the hillock. One of the structures to the south was a *kakoi* (tea room). There was also a detached building where one could enjoy a bath.

Hanabata Residence, Kumamoto Castle.（Eisei bunko）
熊本城花畑屋敷『陽春庭中之図』（永青文庫蔵）

58　城内の御殿・城下の藩士の屋敷-4　大名の遊びの屋敷、ゆとりの建物

　大名の国許の城内の屋敷や江戸の上屋敷は書院造で、障壁画に変化を求める程度で、他藩の大名屋敷のつくりと大きな違いはありません。

　大名たちの教養や趣味を見せたのが、江戸や国許の城下に造った下屋敷です。今も見ることが出来るのが、江戸では後楽園、六義園など、岡山の後楽園、高松の栗林公園、熊本の水前寺公園成趣園、金沢の兼六園などです。武家ではありませんが、京都の桂離宮は、八条宮家の下屋敷です。姫路の殿様は、内郭に、大きな池と築山を築き、数寄屋（茶室）や風呂屋などの建物を設けた向屋敷を造りました。

　向屋敷では、中心に長い炉のある八間四方もある唐傘の間を置き（23頁参照）、池に面した北側の棟の縁から水面に下りる階段を付けています。ここから舟で築山の上の茶屋に向かったのでしょう。南側の棟には、囲（茶室）がありました。其の外、別棟として、風呂を楽しむ建物もありました。（14、15頁参照）

An image of what the *mukai yasiki* of Himezi Castle might have looked like.

姫路城向屋敷の想像図

Castles in Various Areas of Japan

01 Matumae Castle
02 Hakodate Bugyōsyo
03 Hirosaki Castle
04 Yamagata Castle
05 Sendai Castle
06 Siroisi Castle
07 Sirakawa-Komine Castle
08 Aizu-Wakamatu Castle
09 Utunomiya Castle
10 Kōdōkan, Mito Castle
11 Obata-Zinya
12 Kawagoe Castle
13 Edo Castle
14 Sibata Castle
15 Etigo-Takada Castle
16 Kanazawa Castle
17 Maruoka Castle
18 Etizen-Ono castle
19 Remain of Itizyōdani Asakura Castle Town
20 Hukui Castle
21 Ueda Castle
22 Matusiro Castle
23 Matumoto Castle
24 Odawara Castle
25 Sunpu Castle
26 Kakegawa Castle
27 Nagoya Castle
28 Okazaki Castle
29 Inuyama Castle
30 Gihu Castle
31 Ōgaki Castle
32 Hikone Castle
33 Azuti Castle
34 Ōmi-Hatiman Castle
35 Nizyō Castle
36 Osaka Castle
37 Yamato-Kōriyama Castle
38 Wakayama Castle
39 Sasayama Castle
40 Himezi Castle
41 Akasi Castle
42 Ako Castle
43 Bittyū-Matuyama Castle
44 Okayama Castle
45 Tuyama Castle
46 Mihara Castle
47 Hukuyama Castle
48 Hirosima Castle
49 Iwakuni Castle
50 Matue Castle
51 Tuwano Castle
52 Hagi Castle
53 Takamatu Castle
54 Marugame Castle
55 Matuyama Castle
56 Uwazima Castle
57 Ōzu Castle
58 Kōti Castle
59 Nakatu Castle
60 Kokura Castle
61 Hukuoka Castle
62 Karatu Castle
63 Hizen-Nagoya Castle
64 Saga Castle
65 Simabara Castle
66 Kumamoto Castle
67 Hitoyosi Castle
68 Oka Castle
69 Obi Castle
70 Izumi-Humoto
71 Tiran-Humoto
72 Senganen Kagosima
73 Syuri Castle
74 Nakagusuku Castle

各地の城

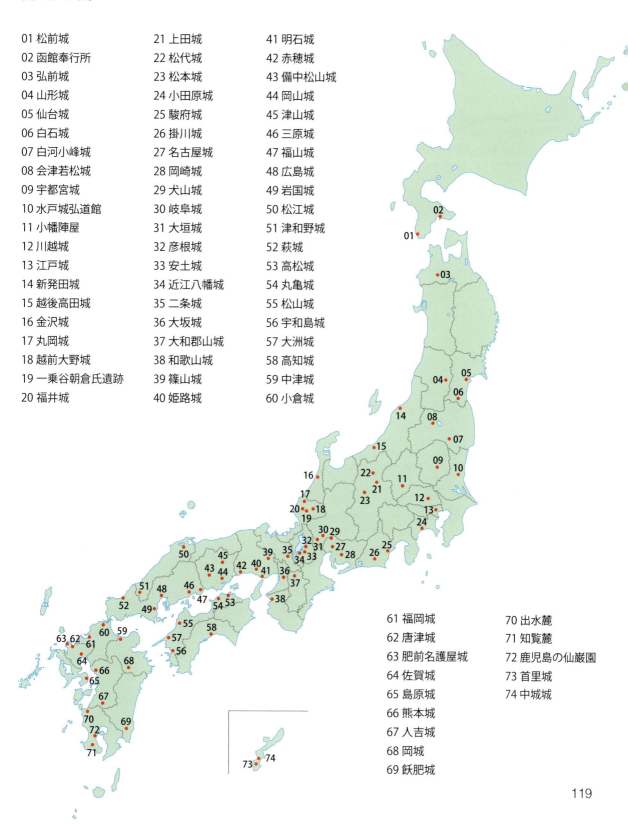

01 松前城
02 函館奉行所
03 弘前城
04 山形城
05 仙台城
06 白石城
07 白河小峰城
08 会津若松城
09 宇都宮城
10 水戸城弘道館
11 小幡陣屋
12 川越城
13 江戸城
14 新発田城
15 越後高田城
16 金沢城
17 丸岡城
18 越前大野城
19 一乗谷朝倉氏遺跡
20 福井城
21 上田城
22 松代城
23 松本城
24 小田原城
25 駿府城
26 掛川城
27 名古屋城
28 岡崎城
29 犬山城
30 岐阜城
31 大垣城
32 彦根城
33 安土城
34 近江八幡城
35 二条城
36 大坂城
37 大和郡山城
38 和歌山城
39 篠山城
40 姫路城
41 明石城
42 赤穂城
43 備中松山城
44 岡山城
45 津山城
46 三原城
47 福山城
48 広島城
49 岩国城
50 松江城
51 津和野城
52 萩城
53 高松城
54 丸亀城
55 松山城
56 宇和島城
57 大洲城
58 高知城
59 中津城
60 小倉城
61 福岡城
62 唐津城
63 肥前名護屋城
64 佐賀城
65 島原城
66 熊本城
67 人吉城
68 岡城
69 飫肥城
70 出水麓
71 知覧麓
72 鹿児島の仙巌園
73 首里城
74 中城城

01 Matumae Castle
　　松前城

Matumae, Hokkaido
北海道松前郡松前町
＜本丸大手門（重要文化財）と復興の天守＞

02-1 Remains of Hakodate Bugyōsyo （Goryokaku）
　　　箱館奉行所跡（五稜郭）

Hakodate, Hokkaido
北海道函館市
＜上空から見た特別史跡・五稜郭の形状＞

02-2 Hakodate Bugyōsyo
　　　箱館奉行所

＜復元された奉行所主要部分＞

02-3 Interior, Hakodate Bugyōsyo
　　　箱館奉行所の内部

＜奉行所表座敷から一の間を見る＞

03-1 Main Gate of Tertiary Enclosure, Hirosaki Castle
弘前城大手門

Hirosaki, Aomori Prefecture
青森県弘前市
＜三の丸の南に位置する大手門（重要文化財）＞

03-2 Donjon, Hirosaki Castle
弘前城天守

＜現存の天守（重要文化財）で「御三階櫓」とよばれた＞

03-3 Samurai Quarter, Hirosaki Castle Town
弘前城下武家屋敷

＜下級武士が居住した旧武家地の仲町（重要伝統的建造物群保存地区）＞

04 East Main Gate, Secondary Enclosure, Yamagata Castle
山形城二の丸東大手門

Yamagata, Yamagata Prefecture
山形県山形市
＜復元された二の丸東大手の桝形門と櫓＞

05 Corner Tower, Sendai Castle
　　仙台城隅櫓

Sendai, Miyagi Prefecture
宮城県仙台市
＜復元された大手門の隅櫓＞

06 Donjon, Siroisi Castle
　　白石城天守

Siroisi, Miyagi Prefecture
宮城県白石市
＜復元された天守（三階櫓）＞

07 Donjon, Sirakawa-Komine Castle
　　白河小峰城天守

Sirakawa, Hukusima Prefecture
福島県白河市
＜復元された天守（三重御櫓）と前御門＞

08 Donjon, Aizu-Wakamatu Castle
　　会津若松城天守

Aizu-Wakamatu, Hukusima Prefecture
福島県会津若松市
＜近年、赤瓦に葺き直された復興の天守＞

09 Remains of Main Enclosure, Utunomiya Castle
宇都宮城本丸跡（一部）

Utunomiya, Totigi Prefecture

栃木県宇都宮市

＜整備後の土塁上に復興された櫓＞

10 Kōdōkan, Mito Castle
水戸城弘道館

Mito, Ibaraki Prefecture

茨城県水戸市

＜旧三の丸に現存する旧弘道館（水戸藩の藩校・特別史跡）の主要部分＞

11 Rakuzan'en, Obata-Zin'ya
小幡陣屋楽山園

Kanra, Gunma Prefecture

群馬県甘楽町

＜発掘後に復元された旧藩主御殿の庭園（名勝）＞

12 Main Residence, Main Enclosure of Kawagoe Castle
川越城本丸表御殿

Kawagoe, Saitama Prefecture

埼玉県川越市

＜現存する本丸表御殿の玄関部分＞

13-1 Foundation of Donjon, Main Enclosure of Edo Castle
江戸城本丸跡の天守台

Tiyoda-ku, Tokyo
東京都千代田区
＜現存する天守台と小天守台の石垣＞

13-2 Remains of Western Enclosure of Edo Castle
江戸城西の丸跡に架かる二重橋

＜現皇居宮殿入口に架かる橋。橋脚が二段構造になっていたことから名付けられ、その名が残る（現在は鉄橋となり下の桁はない）＞

13-3 Soto-Sakurada Gate, Edo Castle
江戸城外桜田門

＜江戸城内郭（特別史跡）の南に造られた桝形形式の城門（重要文化財）＞

13-4 Inner Moats, Edo Castle
江戸城内堀

＜広大な内堀の右側は吹上御苑（現皇居）の土塁＞

14-1 Corner Tower of Secondary Enclosure, Sibata Castle
新発田城旧二の丸隅櫓

14-2 Asigaru Rowhouse, Sibata Castle Town
新発田城下の足軽長屋

Sibata, Niigata Prefecture
新潟県新発田市
＜本丸跡に移築された旧二の丸にあった隅櫓（重要文化財）＞

＜移築整備された旧足軽長屋（重要文化財）＞

15-1 Main Entrance of Main Enclosure, Etigo-Takada Castle
越後高田城本丸大手口

15-2 Temple District, Etigo-Takada Castle Town
越後高田城下の寺町

Zyōetu, Niigata Prefecture
新潟県上越市
＜現存する本丸の堀と土塁＞

＜城下の西に配された寺町＞
浄興寺本堂（重要文化財）

16-1 Caltrop Tower・Gozyukken-Nagaya・Hasizume Gate, Kanazawa Castle
金沢城の菱櫓・五十間長屋・橋爪門と続櫓

Kanazawa, Kanazawa Prefecture
石川県金沢市
＜復元された二の丸大手の門や櫓＞

16-2 Kenrokuen, Kanazawa
金沢城　兼六園

＜金沢城の石川門前に造られた旧城主別邸の大名庭園（特別名勝）にある当時からの噴水＞

16-3 Tyaya-mati, Kanazawa Castle Town
金沢　東山ひがし　茶屋街

＜整備された東山ひがし茶屋町（重要伝統的建造物群保存地区）＞

17 Donjon, Maruoka Castle
丸岡城天守

Sakai, Hukui Prefecture
福井県坂井市
＜初期の様式を伝える現存の天守（重要文化財）＞

18　Etizen-Ōno Castle
　　越前大野城

Ōno, Hukui Prefecture

福井県大野市

＜平山城の山頂に建てられた復興天守＞

19　Remains of Simonokido, Itizyōdani Asakura Castle Town
　　一乗谷朝倉氏遺跡の下城戸跡

Hukui, Hukui Prefecture

＜朝倉氏遺跡（特別史跡）の北端に設けられた城門跡＞

20-1　Foundation of Donjon and Covered Bridge, Hukui Castlecovered
　　福井城の天守台と御廊下橋

Hukui, Hukui Prefecture

福井県福井市

＜内堀に面する天守台の前に架けられた御廊下橋
（復元）＞

20-2　Osensui Residence, Hukui Castle Town
　　福井城下の旧御泉水屋敷

＜復元された旧城主別邸の養浩館（名勝）＞

21-1 Higasi-Koguti, Main Enclosure of Ueda Castle
上田城本丸東虎口

Ueda, Nagano Prefecture

長野県上田市

＜復元された本丸大手門と再移築された両脇(南北)の櫓＞

21-2 Main Gate, Oyakata Residence, Ueda Castle
上田城御屋形表門

＜三の丸跡に残る旧城主御殿の表門(現上田高校内)＞

22-1 Matusiro Castle
松代城跡

Matusiro, Nagano Prefecture

長野県松代市

＜復元された本丸大手の太鼓門桝形と橋＞

22-2 Samurai Residences, Matusiro Castle Town
松代城下の武家屋敷

＜旧武家地の家並＞

23　Donjon, Matumoto Castle
　　松本城天守

Matumoto, Nagano Prefecture

長野県松本市

＜天守群(国宝)の大天守・辰巳附櫓・月見櫓を南からみる＞

24　Donjon, Odawara Castle
　　小田原城天守

Odawara, Kanagawa Prefecture

神奈川県小田原市

＜復興された天守＞

25-1　East Gate of Secondary Enclosure and Moats, Sunpu Castle
　　駿府城二の丸東御門・巽櫓と堀

Sizuoka, Sizuoka Prefecture

静岡県静岡市

＜二の丸東南隅を俯瞰した様子＞

25-2　East Gate of Secondary Enclosure and Tatumi Tower, Sunpu Castle
　　駿府城二の丸東御門と巽櫓

＜復元された巽櫓、二の丸東御門と橋＞

26-1 Residence of Secondary Enclosure, Kakegawa Castle
掛川城二の丸御殿

26-2 Interior of Residence of Secondary Enclosure, Kakegawa Castle
掛川城二の丸御殿の内部

Kakegawa, Sizuoka Prefecture

静岡県掛川市

＜現存する城主の住居であった御殿（重要文化財）＞

＜御書院次の間より上の間をみる＞

27-1 Donjon and South-west Corner Tower, Nagoya Castle
名古屋城天守と未申（西南）隅櫓

27-2 Residence of Main Enclosure, Nagoya Castle
名古屋城本丸御殿玄関

Nagoya, Aiti Prefecture

愛知県名古屋市

＜復興された大・小天守の前面が現存の隅櫓（重要文化財）＞

＜復元された名古屋城（特別史跡）の本丸御殿玄関＞

28 Donjon, Okazaki Castle
　　岡崎城天守

Okazaki, Aiti Prefecture

愛知県岡崎市

＜本丸の復興天守＞

29 Donjon, Inuyama Castle
　　犬山城天守

Inuyama, Aiti Prefecture

愛知県犬山市

＜初期の様式を伝える現存の天守（国宝）＞

30 Remains of Nobunaga Residence, Gihu Castle
　　岐阜城信長居館跡

Gihu City, Gihu Prefecture

岐阜県岐阜市

＜発掘された信長構築の居館跡の石垣＞

31 Main Enclosure of Ōgaki Castle
　　大垣城本丸

Ōgaki, Gihu Prefecture

岐阜県大垣市

＜西門と土塀からみた本丸の天守（いずれも復興）＞

32-1 Distant View of Hikone Castle
　　　彦根城遠望

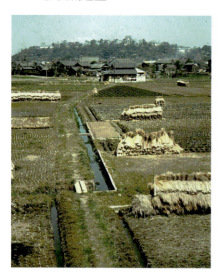

Hikone, Siga Prefecture
滋賀県彦根市
＜遠くに彦根城（特別史跡）の天守がみえる＞

32-2 Donjon, Hikone Castle
　　　彦根城天守

＜本丸に現在も残る天守（国宝）＞

32-3 Genkyūen, Hikone Castle
　　　彦根城玄宮園

＜旧城主別邸の住居部分を後に楽々園と呼ぶようになった。大名庭園（名勝）から見た天守＞

33-1 Fundation of Donjon, Azuti Castle
　　　安土城天守台

Ōmi-Hatiman, Siga Prefecture
滋賀県近江八幡市
＜内側である穴蔵跡より見た現存の安土城（特別史跡）天守台＞

33-2　Main Road, Azuti Castle
　　　安土城の大手道

＜発掘整備された安土城の大手道＞

34-1　Bird's-Eye View of Ōmi-Hatiman Castle Town
　　　近江八幡城下俯瞰

Ōmi-Hatiman, Siga Prefecture
滋賀県近江八幡市
＜八幡山城から見下ろす城下の碁盤目状の町割＞

34-2　Canal, Ōmi-Hatiman Castle Town
　　　近江八幡城下の運河

＜築城と同時に造られた八幡堀とよばれる運河＞

34-3　Matiya, Ōmi-Hatiman Castle Town
　　　近江八幡城下の町屋

＜城下の旧町人地の家並(重要伝統的建造物群保存地区)＞

35-1 East Main gate, Nizyō Castle
二条城の東大手門

Kyoto, Kyoto Prefecture
京都府京都市
＜二条城（世界遺産）の正門にあたる櫓門（重要文化財）＞

35-2 Residence of Secondary Enclosure, Nizyō Castle
二条城二の丸御殿

＜二の丸御殿（国宝）の車寄と遠侍、奥が大広間＞

35-3 Garden of Secondary Enclosure, Nizyō Castle
二条城二の丸庭園

＜御殿の南に広がる庭園（特別名勝）の池と石組＞

35-4 Foundation of Donjon, Nizyō Castle
二条城天守台

＜現在も残る本丸の天守台＞

36-1 Stone Wall, Ōsaka Castle
　　　大坂城石垣の巨石

Ōsaka, Osaka Prefecture
大阪府大阪市
＜本丸大手の桜門桝形に据えられた見付石で蛸石と呼ばれている＞

36-2 Donjon, Ōsaka Castle
　　　大坂城天守

＜豊臣時代の姿を模して江戸時代の天守台に復興された天守＞

36-3 Sixth Tower, Ōsaka Castle
　　　大坂城六番櫓

＜大坂城(特別史跡)の外堀に面した六番櫓(重要文化財)と複雑に屈曲した石垣＞

37 Main Gate and Opposite Tower, Yamato-Kōriyama Castle
　　大和郡山城追手門と向櫓

Yamatokōriyama, Nara Prefecture
奈良県大和郡山市
＜復興された大手の櫓と門＞

38-1 Donjon and coverbridge, Wakayama Castle
和歌山城天守と御橋廊下

Wakayama, Wakayama Prefecture
和歌山県和歌山市
＜復興天守の手前は堀に架かる御橋廊下（復元）＞

38-2 Yōsuien, Wakayama Castle Town
和歌山城下養翠園

＜汐入の庭園（名勝）をもつ旧城主下屋敷＞

39-1 Sasayama Castle
篠山城

Sasayama, Hyōgo Prefecture
兵庫県篠山市
＜広い犬走りをもつ二の丸石垣。内側には復元された大書院が建つ＞

39-2 Samurai Residences, Sasayama Castle Town
篠山城下武家屋敷

＜城下に残る下級武家地の家並（重要伝統的建造物群保存地区）＞

40-1 Distant View of Himezi Castle
姫路城遠望

Himezi, Hyōgo Prefecture
兵庫県姫路市
＜北からみた城郭（世界遺産）と天守群（国宝）＞

40-2 Himezi Castle
姫路城

＜大天守から俯瞰した西の丸の櫓群＞

41 Akasi Castle
明石城

Akasi, Hyōgo Prefecture
兵庫県明石市
＜現存する坤櫓と巽櫓（重要文化財）＞

42 Akō Castle
赤穂城

Akō, Hyōgo Prefecture
兵庫県赤穂市
＜赤穂城の内堀と石垣＞

43 Donjon, Bittyū-Matuyama Castle
備中松山城天守

Takahasi, Okayama Prefecture
岡山県高梁市
＜山城の山頂にある天守（重要文化財）と復元された
櫓および塀＞

44-1 Donjon, Okayama Castle
岡山城天守

Okayama, Okayama Prefecture
岡山県岡山市
＜復興された初期の様式の天守＞

44-2 Moon Viewing Tower, Okayama Castle
岡山城月見櫓

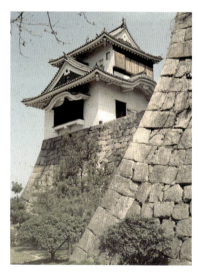

＜本丸北西に現存する月見櫓（重要文化財）＞

44-3 Kōrakuen, Okayama Castle
岡山城　後楽園

＜城の対岸に城主が造った大名庭園（特別名勝）＞

45　Foundation of Donjon, Tuyama Castle
　　津山城天守台

Tuyama, Okayama Prefecture
岡山県津山市
＜天守を櫓や渡櫓が取り囲んでいた様子がわかる石垣の遺構＞

46　Foundation of Donjon, Mihara Castle
　　三原城天守台

Mihara, Hirosima Prefecture
広島県三原市
＜海に面して築かれた城で、天守台に天守は建てられなかった＞

47-1　Husimi Tower, Hukuyama Castle
　　　福山城伏見櫓

Hukuyama, Hirosima Prefecture
広島県福山市
＜本丸大手桝形門に続く伏見櫓（重要文化財）＞

47-2　Donjon, Hukuyama Castle
　　　福山城天守

＜北側の背面からみた復興天守＞

48 Donjon, Hirosima Castle
　　広島城天守

Hirosima, Hirosima Prefecture

広島県広島市

＜二基の小天守が前と横に続いていたが天守のみが復興された＞

49 Foundation of Donjon, Iwakuni Castle
　　岩国城天守台

Iwakuni, Hirosima Prefecture

広島県岩国市

＜今も残る天守台＞

50-1 Donjon, Matue Castle
　　　松江城天守

Matue, Simane Prefecture

島根県松江市

＜正面である南側からみた前面に付櫓をもつ天守(国宝)＞

50-2 Samurai Residences, Matue Castle Town
　　　松江城下武家屋敷

＜城の北に配された旧武家地の家並＞

51　Tuwano Castle
　　　津和野城

Tuwano, Kanoasi-gun, Simane Prefecture
島根県鹿足郡津和野町
＜本丸からみた山城の高石垣＞

52-1　Foundation of Donjon, Hagi Castle
　　　　萩城天守台

Hagi, Yamaguti Prefecture
山口県萩市
＜山城の指月山の前方に構築された天守台と手前に続く石垣＞

52-2　Samurai Residences, Hagi Castle Town
　　　　萩城下武家屋敷

＜旧武家地の家並（重要伝統的建造物群保存地区）＞

52-3　Matiya, Hagi Castle Town
　　　　萩城下の町屋

＜旧町人地に残る往時の商家（史跡萩城下町）＞

53-1 Takamatu Castle
　　　高松城の櫓

53-2 Riturin Park, Takamatu Castle Town
　　　高松城下栗林公園

Takamatu, Kagawa Prefecture
香川県高松市
＜直接海に面していた北の丸月見櫓と手前の水手御門
（いずれも重要文化財）＞

＜旧城主別邸の大名庭園（特別名勝）＞

54-1 Stone Wall and Donjon, Marugame Castle
　　　丸亀城の石垣と天守

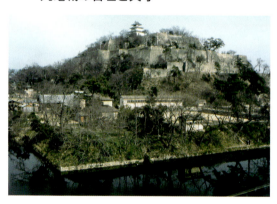

54-2 Main Gate, Marugame Castle
　　　丸亀城大手門

Marugame, Kagawa Prefecture
香川県丸亀市
＜高石垣の城郭の上に建つ現存の天守（重要文化財）＞

＜現存する大手門桝形（重要文化財）、遠方は天守＞

55-1 Donjon, Matuyama Castle
松山城の天守

Matuyama, Ehime Prefecture
愛媛県松山市
＜天守や櫓が建つ本壇(天守郭・重要文化財)の入口＞

55-2 Tower, Matuyama Castle
松山城の櫓

＜大手口の道から復元された本丸太鼓櫓をみる＞

56-1 Donjon, Uwazima Castle
宇和島城天守

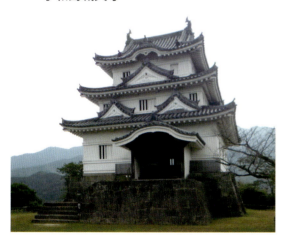

Uwazima, Ehime Prefecture
愛媛県宇和島市
＜本丸に現存する天守(重要文化財)＞

56-2 Noboridati Gate Uwazima Castle
宇和島城上り立ち門

＜城の搦手にあたる場所にたつ現存の薬医門＞

57 Donjon, Ōzu Castle
大洲城天守

Ōzu, Ehime Prefecture

愛媛県大洲市

＜復元された天守と現存の高欄櫓（重要文化財）＞

58-1 Main Gate and Donjon, Kōti Castle
高知城追手門と天守

Kōti, Kōti Prefecture

高知県高知市

＜城の正門である大手の櫓門（重要文化財）＞

58-2 Donjon, Kōti Castle
高知城天守

＜二の丸入口の石段からみた現存天守（重要文化財）の北面＞

58-3 Residence of Main Enclosure (Kaitoku-kan), Kōti Castle
高知城本丸御殿（懐徳館）

＜天守につながる本丸御殿（重要文化財）の玄関式台＞

59 Donjon, Nakatu Castle
　　中津城天守

Nakatu, Ōita Prefecture

大分県中津市

＜実在が不明のまま復興された天守＞

60 Donjon, Kokura Castle
　　小倉城天守

Kitakyūsyū, Hukuoka Prefecture

福岡県北九州市

＜北東からみた復興の天守＞

61 Tower, Hukuoka Castle
　　福岡城の櫓

Hukuoka, Hukuoka Prefecture

福岡県福岡市

＜本丸南西隅の石垣上に建つ祈念櫓＞

62 Donjon, Karatu Castle
　　唐津城天守

Karatu, Saga Prefecture

佐賀県唐津市

＜海岸からみた復興の天守と櫓＞

63-1 Nagoya Castle
名護屋城

Karatu, Saga Prefecture
佐賀県唐津市
＜名護屋城（特別史跡）の天守台付近よりみた遊撃丸跡＞

63-2 Remains of Zin (Encampment), Nagoya Castle
名護屋の陣跡

＜発掘整備された大名堀秀治の陣跡（特別史跡）＞

64-1 Syati Gate, Saga Castle
佐賀城鯱の門

Saga, Saga Prefecture
佐賀県佐賀市
＜本丸表門の鯱の門と続櫓（いずれも重要文化財）＞

64-2 Residence of Main Enclosure, Saga Castle
佐賀城本丸御殿

＜復元された本丸御殿の表向主要部分＞

65-1 Donjon, Simabara Castle
　　島原城天守

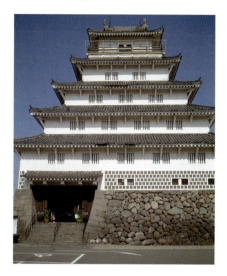

Simabara, Nagasaki Prefecture
長崎県島原市
＜復興された天守＞

65-2 Samurai Residences, Simabara Castle Town
　　島原城下武家屋敷

＜中央に水路が通る旧武家地の家並＞

66-1 Uto Tower, Kumamoto Castle
　　熊本城宇土櫓

Kumamoto, Kumamoto Prefecture
熊本県熊本市
＜熊本城（特別史跡）の本丸北西隅の高石垣上に建つ現存の宇土櫓（重要文化財）＞

66-2 Suizenzi-Syōsyuen, Kumamoto
　　熊本　水前寺成趣園

＜城主が造った御茶屋の大名庭園（名勝）と古今伝授の間＞

67　Hitoyosi Castle
　　人吉城

Hitoyosi, Kumamoto Prefecture
熊本県人吉市
＜復元された多門櫓と長塀＞

68　Stone Wall, Oka Castle
　　岡城の石垣

Takeda, Oita Prefecture
大分県竹田市
＜山城の壮大な高石垣＞

69　Samurai Residences, Obi Castle Town
　　飫肥城下武家屋敷

Nitinan, Miyazaki Prefecture
宮崎県日南市
＜飫肥城近くの旧上級武家地の家並（重要伝統的建造物群保存地区）＞

70　Samurai Residences, Izumi-Humoto
　　出水麓の武家屋敷

Izumi, Kagosima Prefecture
鹿児島県出水市
＜地方支配の拠点であった麓の旧武家地の家並（重要伝統的建造物群保存地区）＞

71 Samurai Residences, Tiran-Humoto
知覧麓の武家屋敷

Minamikyūsyū, Kagosima Prefecture
鹿児島県南九州市
＜生垣が独特な景観をもつ旧武家地の家並（重要伝統的建造物群保存地区）＞

72 Sengan'en, Kagosima
鹿児島 仙巌園

Kagosima, Kagosima Prefecture
鹿児島県鹿児島市
＜城主の別邸だった旧磯庭園（名勝）＞

73 Residence, Syuri Castle
首里城宮殿

Naha, Okinawa Prefecture
沖縄県那覇市
＜復元された首里城跡（世界遺産）の中心建物である正殿＞

74 Nakagusuku Castle
中城城

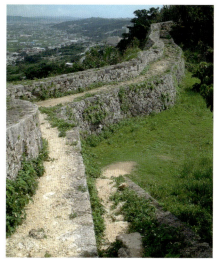

Nakagusuku, Okinawa Prefecture
沖縄県中城村
＜石垣の内側に武者走の石垣を持つ中城城（世界遺産）＞

［掲載図所蔵先］

※図版所蔵先のないものは，すべて著者が所蔵または作図したものである。
※図版の掲載にあたっては，原典および写真に著者が手を加えたものがある。
※写真撮影者の記載のないものは，著者が撮影したものである。

所蔵者：『掲載物（名）』本書のページ

Museum of Asian Art, Berlin：『Kidai Shoran（熙代勝覧）』53
石川県立図書館：『寛文七年金沢図』24
　　　　：『延宝金沢図』37～39
石川県立歴史博物館：『金沢城下図屏風』66
和泉館：『石曳図』46・47
永青文庫：『陽春庭中之図』116
越葵文庫：『福井郭各御門其他見取絵』89
小田原市教育委員会保管：『小田原都市集成図7（史跡・遺構の現況）』40
金沢工業大学増田達男研究室・金沢城調査研究所木越隆三共同制作：金沢城下寛文七年身分別配置図-現代地図重図 25
国土地理院ウェブサイト（CKK80-3 CIA11, 12）：姫路市空中写真（1980.10）27
国立国会図書館：『中村座内外の図』60
国立歴史民俗博物館：『江戸図屏風』72
榊神社蔵榊原家史料（旧高田藩和親会管理）：『高田城絵図』41
静嘉堂文庫：『駿府図』34
高田開府400年祭実行委員会：『CG・大手橋からみた高田城の姿』41
竹田市教育委員会：『御城真景図』29
竹中大工道具館：『大工道具13種（四ツ目錐を除く）』108,109
都立中央図書館特別文庫室：『江戸城御本丸万延度御普請御殿向表奥惣絵図』113
　　　　：『御本丸大広間地絵図』96
　　　　：『御本丸大広間南御入側より御上段後御入側』96
　　　　：『御本丸大広間南面建地割五十分ノ一』97
　　　　：『御本丸大広間足堅絵図』98
　　　　：『御本丸大広間格天井惣絵図』99
　　　　：『御本丸大広間御屋根水取絵図』99
　　　　：『御本丸大広間小屋梁配絵図』99
名古屋城総合事務所：『風俗図』（部分）62
名古屋市博物館：『築城図屏風』（部分）48
姫路市：『姫路城旧天守の推定復元模型』64
　　　　：『姫路市都市計画図』4
　　　　：姫路城大天守地下旧礎石配置図（『姫路城保存修理報告書Ⅲ（本文）』より作図）65
姫路市立城郭研究室：『姫路御城廻侍屋鋪新絵図』18
　　　　：『姫路侍屋敷図』20
福井県教育委員会保管：『一乗谷朝倉氏遺跡遺構』30
　　　　：一乗谷朝倉氏遺跡現状空中写真 31
松本市：『国宝　松本城（解体・調査編）』「天守石垣根石及び地形胴木を望む」51
大谷信一：『姫路城図屏風』36
笠松雅弘：一乗谷朝倉氏遺跡武家屋敷地区 30,103
　　　　：一乗谷朝倉氏遺跡町屋地区 30
　　　　：一乗谷朝倉氏遺跡町屋地区 30
　　　　：一乗谷朝倉氏遺跡板葺屋根 103
澤崎明治：南側より見た姫路城 5
中根忠之：『播州姫路城図』2
橋本正次旧蔵：姫路城三の丸御居城御殿平面図の内鶴の間 13
藤岡通夫：津山城天守東面復元立面図 83

（転載）

『日本建築史基礎資料集成14（城郭1）』：犬山城天守南面立面図 80
　　　　：丸岡城平面図（一階）50

（「各地の城」の撮影者）

浅野伸子：05, 11, 13-1, 14-1・2, 20-2, 22-1・2, 25-1, 28, 30, 31, 32-3, 33-2, 34-1・2・3, 35-1, 36-1・2・3, 37, 38-2, 39-1・2, 42, 43, 44-1・2, 45, 47-1・2, 49, 50-1・2, 51, 52-1, 54-2, 55-1, 56-1, 57, 58-2・3, 62, 63-1・2, 69, 70
小粥祐子：13-3
函館市：02-1
佐々木修：18
笠松雅弘：19
澤崎明治：56-2
服部佐智子：27-2

Index and Glossary

A

Aizu-wakamatu Castle 122
Akasi Castle 137
approach 38
arch 50
arrowport 86
artisans 21
attached tower 72
audience hall 62
Azuti Castle 132, 133

B

back filling 46
balustrade 82
ban'ya 52
Base stone 85
bath 13
bath house 15, 62
Bittyū-Matuyama Castle ... 28, 138
book of military strategy ... 68, 70
bottom rock 50
built-in desk 110

C

caltrop gate 11, 15, 16
canal 24
carpenter's tool 108
castle town .... 19, 35~45, 52
central pillar 85
Cherry Gate 16
clay tile 102
clay wall 100
corridor 11, 74
Crane Room 13
cusped arch window 82

D

daidokoro 11, 76
daitensyu 9

defensive perimeter 24
defensive perimeter moat ... 22
donjon .... 5, 50, 72~77
dormer gable 80
Dowry Tower 11
dozō 11

E

earthwork 19, 22, 42
Edo Castle 42, 112, 124
empty moat 22, 40
enclosure 5
entrance hall 13
Etigo-Takada Castle 125
Etizen-Ōno Castle 127

F

Fifty Bay yagura 46, 126
fire watchtower 54
folding screen 66
food preparation room .. 13

G

gabled roof 88
garden 30
garden enclosure 7
gate guard 52
genkan 11
Gihu Castle 46, 126, 131
Gozyukken Yagura 46
great defensive perimeter ... 40
guard station 52
gunport 86

H

Hagi Castle 141
Hakodate Bugyōsyo 120
Hanzōmon 42
heizyūmon 88, 90
Higasi Tyaya district ... 62, 126

highway 21, 36
Hikone Castle 82, 132
hill-on-the-plain castle ... 7, 26
Himezi Castle ... 3, 64, 74, 137
Hirai Castle 28
hirayamaziro 7, 26
hiraziro 32
hiroma 11
Hirosaki Castle 102, 121
Hirosima Castle 140
Hitoyosi Castle 148
hiyoku irimoya 80
honmaru 5
hori 5
house of artisan 30
Hukui Castle 32, 127
Hukuoka Castle 145
Hukuyama Castle 139
huroya 62

I

idonokuruwa 7
Iidabasi 42
inner enclosure ... 3, 5, 7, 19
inuinokuruwa 7
Inuyama Castle 72, 131
irimoya 80
isigaki 5
isiotosi 86
Itigaya 42
Itizyōdani 28, 30
Itizyōdani Asakura Castle Town
.... 127
Iwakuni Castle 140
Izumi-Humoto 148

K

kabuki play 60
kabukimon 88, 90

153

Kaga guti Gate ········· 32, 89
Kakegawa Castle ············ 130
Kaminokido ···················30
Kanazawa ······19, 23, 36, 38
Kanazawa Castle
·········24, 46, 102, 126
karabori ························22
Karakasa no Ma ······· 15, 116
Karatu Castle ············· 145
katō mado ·····················82
Kawagoe Castle ············ 123
Kenrokuen ···················· 126
kesyō yagura ·················11
Kidaisyōran ···················52
kido ·····························52
kidoban ························52
Kiku-zyutu ····················92
kirikomi-hagi ·················48
kitchen ······· 9, 11, 13, 76
kiwari-zyutu ··················92
Kōdōkan ······················ 123
Kokura Castle ·············· 145
kōraimon ······················88
kotensyu ·······················9
Kōti Castle ··················· 144
Kumamoto Castle ···44, 100, 147
Kuratuki Canal ···············24
Kuratuki Yōsui ················24
Kurosyoin ···················· 112

L

large outer defensive perimeter ···19
lookout ·······················76
lord of the castle ············13
Lower Gate ···················30

M

main donjon ········· 9, 74, 76
main enclosure ················5
Marugame Castle ············ 142
Maruoka Castle ···50, 102, 126

masugata-type gate ··········56
matiya ·························66
Matue Castle ·········· 72, 140
Matumae Castle ········ 46, 120
Matumoto Castle ··· 32, 74, 129
Matusiro Castle ············· 128
Matuyama Castle ········ 74, 143
mawaributai ···················60
metal shingle ················ 102
middle enclosure ·············19
Mihara Castle ··············· 139
minor donjon ···················9
mituke ·························52
moat ················ 5, 22, 40
Morisada mankō ···············62
mountain castle ···············28
mounted exit ··················32
mukai yasiki ···················15
munahuda ·····················46
munamon ················ 88, 90
Musasino Residence ··········16

N

nagatubone ···················30
Nagaya ························58
Nagoya Castle ·········· 62, 130
nakakuruwa ···················19
Nakagusuku Castle ·········· 149
Nakane drawing ············3, 5
Nakatu Castle ··············· 145
nawabari ······················70
neisi ···························50
New Syoin ···················13
ninomaru ·······················7
nisinomaru ·····················5
Nizyo Castle ·········· 112, 134
nizyū-yagura ···················5
Nō stage ················ 13, 60
northwestern enclosure ········7
nozura-zumi ···················48

O

Obata-Zinya ················· 123
Obi Castle town ············· 148
odaidokoro ·····················9
Odawara Castle ········ 22, 129
Ōgaki Castle ················ 131
Oka Castle ············· 28, 148
Okayama Castle ············· 138
Okazaki Castle ··············· 131
ōkido ··························52
okosiezu ·······················96
Ōmi-Hatiman Castle town ··· 133
opposite estate ···············15
oryōri-no-ma ···················9
Ōsaka Castle ················ 135
Ōzu Castle ··················· 144
outer enclosure ···············19

P

paired wing hip-and-gable ······80
place for construction work
························· 5, 16
plain castle ············ 32, 40
plan ························· 114
plaster ······················ 100
plastered wall ··········76, 82
post-and-beam construction ···98
preparation room for side dishes
···························9

Q

quarry ························46

R

reception hall ················11
red tile ····················· 102
Remains of Hakodate Bugyōsyo
························· 120
residence ·····················11
residence of the main enclosure ···26
revolving stage ···············60

ridge plate ·················46
rope stretching ·················70
rowhouse ·················58

S

Saga Castle ················· 146
Sakura no Mon ·················16
sakuziba ·················5, 7, 16
samurai quarter ·················35
samurai residence ····· 30, 114
sandō ·················38
sangi-zumi ·················48
sannomaru ················· 5
Sasayama Castle ················· 136
sasizu ·················94
secondary enclosure ················· 7
seizing land ·················68
Sendai Castle ················· 122
seri ·················60
shōgun ·················11
shuden style ················· 112
sibaigoya ·················60
Sibata Castle ················· 125
Simabara Castle ················· 147
simonokido ·················30
Sirakawa-komine Castle ····· 122
Siroisi Castle ················· 122
sirosyoin ················· 112
sōgamae-bori ·················22
sotoguruwa ·················19
sotosōgamae ·················19
stable ·················30
staggered shelves ················· 110
stone tile ················· 102
stone wall ·················5, 44
stone-drop ·················86
storehouse ·················11
sukiya ·················13
Sunpu ·················35
Sunpu Castle ·················102, 129
syoin-style ·················110, 112

syoin-zukuri ················· 110
Syuri Castle ················· 149

T

taimenzyo ·················62
Takada Castle ·················40
Takahasi ·················28
Takamatu Castle ················· 142
tamon-yagura ················· 5
Tatumi Canal ·················24
tea room ·················13
temple district ·················21, 38
temple ·················21, 38
tensyu ················· 5
teppōzama ·················86
tera mati ·················21, 38
tertiary enclosure ··· 5, 12〜17
theater ·················60
three-dimensional model ·········96
three-story yagura ·················78
tidorihahu ·················80
tigaidana ················· 110
Tiger Room ·················13
Tiran-Humoto ················· 149
tokonoma ·········9, 110, 114
Tora no Ma ·················13
townhouse ·················66
tozama daimyō ·················68
trapdoor ·················60
tubone ················· 9
tuke-syoin ················· 110
tuke-yagura ·················72
tukimi tower ·················74
Tunegoten ·················30
Turu no Ma ·················13
Tuwano Castle ················· 141
Tuyama Castle ················· 139
two-story tower ·········5, 85
tyōdaigamae ················· 110
tyōnin ·················21

U

Ueda Castle ·················85, 128
umadasi ·················32
umaya ·················30
Umbrella Room ·········15, 116
upper gate ·················30
urban commoner ·················21
utikomi-hagi ·················48
utikuruwa ·················19
Utunomiya Castle ····· 88, 123
Uwazima Castle ················· 143
uzumimon ·················88, 90

W

Wakayama Castle ················· 136
watari-yagura ·················74
water supply ·················58
well ·················58
well enclosure ················· 7
western enclosure ················· 5
women attendant ·················30
wooden pile ·················50

Y

yaguramon ·················88
yakuimon ·················90
Yamagata Castle ················· 121
Yamato-Kōriyama Castle ··· 135
yamazatokuruwa ················· 7
yamaziro ·················28, 30
yazama ·················86

Z

zidori ·················68
zitinsai ················· 106
zyōdan-no-ma ·················9, 110
zyōka mati ·················19
zyōtōsai ················· 106

［索引 専門用語］

※数値の黒文字は本文の項目番号
※数値の赤文字は図版のある項目番号

［あ行］

あかかべ　赤壁 ……………………………… 57
あかがわら，—ぶき　赤瓦，—葺 ………… 51,51
あくただめ　芥溜 …………………………… 29,29
あしがためえず　足堅絵図 ………………… 48,49
ありかべ，—なげし　蟻壁，—長押 …… 46,55,46,55
いしおとし　石落し ………………………… 43,43
いしがき，石垣 ……………………… 22〜25,22,24
いしがわら，—ぶき　石瓦，—葺 ………… 51,51
いしきりば　石切り場 ……………………… 23
いしどい　石樋 ……………………………… 28
いしびき　石曳 ……………………………… 23
いたぶき　板葺 ……………………………… 51,51
いっすんけい　一寸計 ……………………… 47,48
いとまき，—じょう　糸巻，—状 ………… 25
いぬいのこてんしゅ　乾小天守 ………… 38,37,38
いましょいん　居間書院 …………………… 55
いりもや　入母屋 ………………………… 40,40,52
うずみもん　埋門 …………………………… 44,45
うちぐるわ　内郭 ……………… 1,2,3,9,17,22,2
うちこみはぎ　打込はぎ …………………… 24,24
うちのりなげし　内法長押 ………………… 46,55
うまだし　馬出し …………………………… 16,44
うみじろ　海城 ……………………………… 16
うらごめ　裏込め …………………………… 23
うらながや　裏長屋 ………………………… 29
うわぬり　上塗 ……………………………… 50,50
おおかべ　大壁 ……………………………… 50
おおきど　大木戸 …………………………… 26,28
おおじょいん　大書院 ……………………… 55,55
おおびき　大引 ……………………………… 48
おおひろま　大広間 ………………………… 48,56,48
おおむね　大棟 …………………………… 41,52,52
おが　大鋸 …………………………………… 54,54
おく　奥 ……………………………………… 55,57
おこざしき　御小座敷 ……………………… 56
おこしえず　起絵図 ………………………… 48
おしいた　押板 ……………………………… 55,55
おとこゆ　男湯 ……………………………… 31
おとしがけ　落掛 …………………………… 46,55
おにがわら　鬼瓦 ………………………… 48,52,52
おの　斧 ……………………………………… 54,54
おもて　表 ………………………………… 55,57,56

おもてもん　表門 …………………………… 55,55
おりあげごうてんじょう　折上格天井 …… 55

［か行］

かきえず　書絵図 …………………………… 47,47
かけひ　懸樋。掛樋 ………………………… 28,28
かけや　掛矢 ………………………………… 54
かこい　囲 …………………………………… 58
かすがい　鎹 ………………………………… 23,54
かとうまど　火灯窓 ………………………… 41
かなづち　金槌 ……………………………… 54
かねじゃく　曲尺 ………………………… 54,54
かぶきしばい　歌舞伎芝居 ………………… 30
かぶき，—もん　冠木，—門 …………… 44,45,45
かべ　壁 ……………………… 38,49,50,57,50
かみのきど　上城戸 ………………………… 15,15
かみやしき　上屋敷 ………………………… 55
かもい　鴨居 ……………………………… 46,48,49
からはふ　唐破風 ……………………… 52,42,52
かんきゃくせき　観客席 …………………… 30
かんじょうかた　勘定方 …………………… 48
かんな　鉋 ………………………………… 54,54
かんのんびらき　観音開き ………………… 44,45
きくじゅつ　規矩術 ………………………… 46
ぎしき　儀式 ………………………………… 53
きじゅん　基準 …………………………… 55,57,57
きじゅんすんぽう　基準寸法 ……………… 46
きたのこてんしゅ　北小天守 ……………… 38
きど　木戸 …………………………………… 26,26
ぎょしんのま　御寝の間 …………………… 55
きりこみはぎ　切込はぎ …………………… 24,24
きりづま，—やね　切妻，—屋根 ……… 44,45,52
きわり　木割 ……………………………… 46,46
ぎんみかた　吟味方 ………………………… 48
くい　杭 …………………………………… 25,54
くぎぬき　釘抜き …………………………… 54
くぐり，—とびら　潜り，—扉 …………… 26,44
くだりむね　下り棟 ……………………… 52,52
くるわ　郭 ………………………… 2,3,16,35,46,1
くろしょいん　黒書院 ……………………… 56
くわはじめ　鍬始 …………………………… 53
ぐんがくしょ　軍学書 …………………… 35,35
げきじょう　劇場 …………………………… 30
げぎょ　懸魚 ………………………………… 48
けこみ　蹴込 ………………………………… 46
げすいみぞ　下水溝 ………………………… 29,29
げんかん　玄関 …………………………… 55,55
けんざお　間竿 ……………………………… 54

けんちくこうじ	建築工事	46〜54
けんちくずめん	建築図面	47,48
げんのう	玄能	54,54
こうか	後架	29,29
こうぞう	構造	39〜42,53
ごうてんじょう	格天井	49,55
こうらいもん	高麗門	44,44,45
こかべ	小壁	46
ごきゅうそく	御休息	56
こぐち	虎口	35
こけら	柿	50
ござのま	御座之間	48,55
こしだかしょうじ	腰高障子	55
こしょいん	小書院	55,55
こてんしゅ	小天守	4,13,38
こてんしゅだい	小天守台	36
こひろま	小広間	56
こまい,―だけ	小舞,―竹	50,50
こやぐみ	小屋組	48
こやばりくばりえず	小屋梁配絵図	49

[さ行]

さおぶちてんじょう	棹縁天井	57
さくじ	作事	46,53
さくじかた	作事方	48
さくじば	作事場	8,46,1,8
ざくろぐち	ざくろ口	31
さしず	指図	47,48,47
さんぎづみ	算木積	24
さんじゅうやぐら	三重櫓	14,39
さんのまる	三の丸	2,3,46
さんのまるごきょじょう	三の丸御居城	6,1,6
さんのまるむかいやしき	三の丸向屋敷	7,1,7
じいん	寺院	10,17
じえず	地絵図	48,48
じぎょうえず	地形絵図	48
しきい	敷居	41,46,48,49
しきばり	敷梁	48
しきゃくもん。よつあしもん	四脚門	45,45
じぎょう	地形	25
じくぐみ,―こうほう	軸組,―構法	49
ししゃのま	使者の間	55
じしんばんしょ	自身番所	27
しせつ	施設	44,45
したじ	下地	49〜51
したぬり	下塗	50,50
じちんさい	地鎮祭	53
しっくい	漆喰	50
じどり	地取り	34
しばいごや	芝居小屋	30
しぶいち	四分一	50
しもながし	下流し	29
しものきど	下城戸	15,15
しもやしき	下屋敷	58
しゃくだにいし	笏谷石	51
しゃち	鯱	52,42,52
しゅくしゃく	縮尺	47
しゅでんけいしき	主殿形式	56
しゅら	修羅	23
しょいん	書院	55,57,55
しょいんづくり	書院造	55,56,58,55
じょうかまち	城下町	9〜10,15,17〜22,26〜31,33,55,57,17
じょうすいどう	上水道	28
じょうだんのま	上段の間	55,55
じょうだんかまち	上段框	55
じょうとうさい	上棟祭	53
じょうないのごてん	城内の御殿	55〜58
しょうにん	商人	17
しょうへきが	障壁画	58
じょうほう	定法	57
しょくにん	職人	17
しりょう	史料	57
しりん	支輪	55
しるし	印	54
しろ	城	32〜39,44,46,51,52
しろいかべ。しらかべ	白い壁,白壁	50
しろしょいん	白書院	48,56
しろつち,―ぬり	白土,―塗	41,50
しんかべ	真壁	50
しんばしら	心柱	42
すいどう	水道	28,29
すきや	数寄屋	58
すさ	苆	50,50
すみさし	墨差し	54,54
すみつぼ	墨壺	54,54
すみむね	隅棟	40,52,52
ずめん	図面	47,48
せいすん	正寸	48
せきひ。いしどい	石樋	28
せり	迫	30
せんとう	銭湯	31
そうがまえ,―ぼり	総構,―堀	11,12,17
そとぐるわ	外郭	9,10,33
そとそうがまえ	外総構	20

[た行]

- だいがいかく　大外郭 …………………………… 11,20,20
- だいぎり　台切 ………………………………………… 54
- だいく　大工 …………………………………… 33,46,53
- だいくどうぐ　大工道具 …………………………… 54
- だいくまち　大工町 ………………………………… 33
- だいてんしゅ　大天守 ………………………… 4,38,37,40
- だいとうりょう　大棟梁 …………………………… 48
- だいどころ　台所 …………………………… 29,38,55,57,55
- だいみょうやしき　大名屋敷 ……………………… 55
- たたきのみ　叩き鑿 ………………………………… 54
- たてじわり　建地割 ……………………………… 48,48
- たもんやぐら　多聞櫓 …………………………… 2,39,44,46
- ちがいだな　違棚 …………………………… 55,57,46,55
- ちくひ。たけどい　竹樋 …………………………… 28
- ちけい　地形 ………………………………………… 35
- ちどりはふ　千鳥破風 …………………………… 40,52,40,42
- ちゃしつ　茶室 ……………………………………… 46,58
- ちゃや　茶屋 ………………………………………… 58
- ちょうだいがまえ　帳台構 ……………………… 48,55,55
- ちょうな　手斧 …………………………………… 53,54,54
- ちょうなおさめ　手斧納 …………………………… 53
- ちょうなはじめ　手斧始 …………………………… 53
- ちょうにんち　町人地 ……………………………… 26
- つかばしら　束柱 …………………………………… 49
- つきのみ　突き鑿 …………………………………… 54
- つきみやぐら　月見櫓 ……………………………… 37
- つけしょいん　付書院 ……………………………… 55
- つけやぐら　付櫓 ………………………………… 36,36
- つじばんしょ　辻番所 ……………………………… 27
- つちかべ　土壁 ……………………………………… 50
- つちがわら　土瓦 …………………………………… 51
- ていえん　庭園 …………………………………… 28,56
- ていかくしき　梯郭式 ……………………………… 35
- てっぽうざま　鉄砲狭間 ………………………… 43,43
- てらまち　寺町 …………………………………… 10,19
- てんしゅ　天守 ………………… 9,13,14,25,36～43,46,50,52
- てんしゅぐるわ　天守郭 …………………………… 4
- てんしゅぐん　天守群 …………………………… 2,38
- てんしゅだい　天守台 …………………………… 32,36
- てんじょう　天井 ………………………………… 48,57
- てんじょうえず　天井絵図 ……………………… 48,49
- てんじょうなげし　天井長押 …………………… 46,55
- といし　砥石 ……………………………………… 54,54
- どうがわらぶき　銅瓦葺 …………………………… 51
- どうじょう　道場 …………………………………… 19
- どうひ。どうとい　銅樋 …………………………… 28
- とうりょう　棟梁 …………………………………… 53
- とこ,―のま　床,―の間 …………………………… 55,57,55
- とこおしいた　床押板 ……………………………… 46
- どぞう　土蔵 ………………………………………… 50
- とびら　扉 ………………………………………… 44,45
- とりぶすま　鳥衾 …………………………………… 52
- どるい　土塁 …………………… 9,11,17,21,26,35,42,21

[な行]

- なかおく　中奥 ……………………………………… 56
- なかぐるわ　中郭 ………………………………… 9,10,17
- なかにわ　中庭 …………………………………… 37,38
- なかぬり　中塗 ……………………………………… 50
- ながや　長屋 ……………………………………… 29,57
- なかやしき　中屋敷 ………………………………… 55
- ながやもん　長屋門 ………………………………… 55
- なげし　長押 ……………………………………… 48,55
- なんばんもじり　南蛮捻り ………………………… 54
- なまり,―がわらぶき　鉛,―瓦葺 ………………… 51,51,52
- なわばり　縄張り ………………………………… 35,46
- にしのこてんしゅ　西小天守 ………………… 32,38,37,38
- にしのまる　西の丸 ……………………………… 2,3,5
- にじゅうやぐら　二重櫓 …………………………… 4,4
- にのまる　二の丸 ………………………………… 3,46
- にのまるごてん　二の丸御殿 …………………… 56,56
- にぶけい　二分計 …………………………………… 47
- ぬき　貫 ……………………………………………… 50
- ぬりごめかべ　塗籠壁 ……………………………… 41
- ねいし　根石 ………………………………………… 25
- のうぶたい　能舞台 ………………………………… 30
- のうみん　農民 ……………………………………… 17
- のこぎり　鋸 ……………………………………… 54,54
- のづらづみ　野面積 …………………………… 24,36,24
- のみ　鑿 ……………………………………………… 54

[は行]

- はくろう　白鑞 ……………………………………… 51
- はしら　柱 …………………………………………… 53
- はしらはり　柱梁 …………………………………… 49
- はしらますんぽう　柱間寸法 ……………………… 48
- はしらめん　柱面 …………………………………… 46
- はしらめんうち　柱面内 …………………………… 46
- はしらめんおもて　柱面表 ………………………… 46
- はり　梁 …………………………………………… 42,49
- はりえず　貼絵図 …………………………………… 47
- はりつけかべ　張付壁 …………………………… 50,55
- はんしのやしき　藩士の屋敷 …………………… 55～58
- ばんしょ　番所 ……………………………………… 26
- ばんや　番屋 ………………………………………… 26

見出し	漢字	ページ
ひがしのこてんしゅ	東小天守	38,37,38
ひきつけいた	引き付け板	46
ひのみだい	火の見台	27
ひのみやぐら	火の見櫓	27,27
ひよくいりもや	比翼入母屋	40,40,42
ひらいり	平入り	44,45
ひらじろ	平城	16,20,16
ひらどま	平土間	30
ひらやまじろ	平山城	3,13
ひろま	広間	55,55
ひろみ	広見	18,31,18
ぶけち	武家地	17
ぶけやしき	武家屋敷	15,27,55,57,15,17,57
ふしん	普請	32,46
ぶたい	舞台	30
ふのり	布海苔	50
ふろ	風呂	55
ふろや	風呂屋	31,58,31
ふんすい	噴水	12
へい	塀	21,43〜45
へいじゅうもん	塀重門	44,45,45
へいほう	兵法	46
へいめん	平面	56,57
へいめんず	平面図	31,47,48,57,31,36,42,56
へら	箆	47
べんがら	弁柄	50,51
べんじょ	便所	29
ほうぎょう	方形。宝形	52
ぼうろう	望楼	38,40,41
ほったて	掘立て	49
ほり	堀	9,11,16,20,21,26,28,35,44,1,21
ほんがわら，―ぶき	本瓦，―葺	51,52
ほんまる	本丸	2〜4,35,36,46,20
ほんまるごてん	本丸御殿	13,16,22,50,56,56
ほんまるのごてん	本丸の御殿	4

[ま行]

見出し	漢字	ページ
まいぎり	舞錐	54
まえびき	前挽	54,54
ますがた	枡形	44,22,44
ますがたもん	枡形門	28
まちや	町屋	18,15,17,33
まるがわら	丸瓦	52
まわりぶたい	回り舞台	30
みずうり	水売り	29
みずほり	水堀	9,11
みせ	店	10,18
みつけ	見付	26

見出し	漢字	ページ
みつめぎり	三つ目錐	54
むかいやしき	向屋敷	7,58,58
むしぶろ	蒸し風呂	31
むなぎ	棟木	49,53
むなづか	棟束	53
むなもん。むなかど	棟門	44,45,45
むね	棟	45,48,52,58
めつけかた	目付方	48
もくひ。きどい	木樋	28
もちまき	餅撒き	53
ものみ	物見	40
もや	母屋	48,49
もん	門	26,38,44,45,57

[や行]

見出し	漢字	ページ
や	矢	43,53
やあな	矢穴	23
やくいもん	薬医門	45,45
やぐら	櫓	25,39〜43,46,50,53,43
やぐらもん	櫓門	44
やざま	矢狭間	43
やね	屋根	30,38,40,45,49〜53,50,52
やねざい	屋根材	47
やねみずとりえず	屋根水取絵図	48,49
やまじろ	山城	14,15
やりがんな	鐁鉋。槍鉋	54
ゆぶね	湯船	31
ゆみ	弓	43,53
ゆや	湯屋	31
ようすい	用水	12
よくそう	浴槽	31
よせむね	寄棟	40,52
よつめぎり	四ツ目錐	54

[ら行]

見出し	漢字	ページ
りっちゅう	立柱	53
りょうりのま　お―	御―料理の間	4,6,4,55
りんかくしき	輪郭式	35
れんりつてんしゅぐん	連立天守群	37
ろくだか	禄高	55
ろくぶけい	六部計	47

[わ行]

見出し	漢字	ページ
わたりやぐら	渡櫓	37,38
わらずさ	藁苆	50

[索引　城]

※各地の城は119頁の一覧表を参照してください。
※数値の黒文字は本文の項目番号
※数値の赤文字は図版のある項目番号

[あ行]

犬山城天守……………………………………36,40,40
一乗谷朝倉氏遺跡………………………………14,15,15
　　朝倉氏館．湯殿庭園．諏訪庭園．一乗谷川
上田城本丸西櫓…………………………………42,42
　　武家屋敷………………………………………57,57
宇都宮城枡形……………………………………………44
宇和島藩江戸中屋敷……………………………………55
江戸城………………………………21,44,48,49,21,23,53,56
　　天守………………………………………36,40,36,48
　　本丸、本丸御殿…………………………28,56,47,56
　　上棟式、手斧納式、餅蒔き……………………………53
　　北桔橋…………………………………………………28
　　西の丸水道……………………………………………28
江戸城下町……6,27,28,29,30,31,55,56,58,27,28,29,30,31,55
　　芝居小屋……………………………………………30,30
　　　中村座．市村座
　　見付（大木戸．木戸）……………………………26,26
　　　四谷大木戸………………………………………28
　　自身番所……………………………………………27,27
　　半蔵門………………………………………………21
　　火の見櫓……………………………………………27,27
　　神田上水，懸樋……………………………………28,28
　　水道橋………………………………………………28,28
　　目白下大洗堰………………………………………28
　　後楽園………………………………………………58
　　六義園………………………………………………58
大坂城天守……………………………………………36
大洲城…………………………………………………52
岡城（大分県竹田市）………………………………14,14
岡山城後楽園…………………………………………58
小田原城大外郭……………………………………11,20,20

[か行]

金沢城…………………………………22,23,51,24,51,52
　　石川門……………………………………………22,44
　　兼六園……………………………………………12,58

金沢城下町……………………12,18,19,20,33,34,12,18,19,33,34
　　犀川、一大橋……………………………………11,12,19,33,33
　　浅野川、一大橋…………………………………11,12,19
　　鞍月用水…………………………………………12
　　辰巳用水…………………………………………12,20
　　北国街道…………………………………………19,33
　　尾山神社…………………………………………12
　　東茶屋街…………………………………………31
熊本城…………………………………………………22
　　本丸御殿…………………………………………22,50
　　宇土櫓……………………………………………39
　　花畑屋敷…………………………………………58
　　水前寺誠趣園……………………………………58
小倉城…………………………………………………41
五稜郭…………………………………………………35

[さ行]

駿府城天守……………………………………………51
駿府城下町……………………………………………17,17

[た行]

高田城…………………………………………20,21,20
高梁→備中松山城
高松城　栗林公園……………………………………58
長州藩江戸上屋敷……………………………………55
津山城天守……………………………………………41
鳥羽城…………………………………………………16

[な行]

名古屋城………………………………………17,31,51
　　天守………………………………………………51
　　本丸御殿対面所障子……………………………31,31
　　　名古屋城下町…………………………………17
二条城二の丸御殿……………………………………56,56

161

[は行]

彦根城
 天守 …………………………………………… 41,41
 天秤櫓 …………………………………………… 39
備中松山城 ………………………………………… 14
 臥牛山 …………………………………………… 14
 城下町 …………………………………………… 14,14
姫路城 ……………………………………………… 13,34,02
 羽柴秀吉の姫路城 ……………………………… 32,32
 黒田官兵衛の姫路城 …………………………… 32,34
 内郭 ……………………………………………
  …… 01,02,03,04,05,06,07,08,09,22,01,02,03,04,05,06,07,08
  天守郭 ………………………………………… 04,02
  天守 …………… 03,04,09,13,32,37,38,42,13,32,37,38,40,42,52
  本丸 …………………………………………… 03,04,02,03
   本丸御殿 …………………………………… 13
  菱の門 ………………………………………… 05,07,08
  三国掘（池）………………………………… 05,06,02
  西の丸 ………………………………………… 03,05,03,05
   御殿 ………………………………………… 05
   化粧櫓 ……………………………………… 05
  二の丸 ………………………………………… 03
  三の丸 ………………………………………… 03,08,13
   御居城（西屋敷）………………………… 06,02,03,06
    鶴の間,虎の間
   向屋敷 ……………………………………… 07,58,02,03
    唐笠間 ………………………………… 07,58,07
   武蔵野御殿 ………………………………… 08,03
   御作事場 …………………………………… 03,08,02,03,08
    絵図所,絵図小屋,大工小屋,瓦小屋,左官小屋,
    材木小屋,板小屋,すさ小屋,縄小屋,藁小屋,釜屋
姫路城下町 ………………………………………… 09,33,18,33
 中郭（中曲輪）………………………………… 09,10,11
 外郭（外総構）………………… 09,10,11,18,22,09,10,11,18,22
平井城 ……………………………………………… 14
弘前城 ……………………………………………… 51
福井城 ……………………………………………… 16,51
天守、本丸 ………………………………………… 16
福井城下町 ………………………………………… 16,16
 舎人門 …………………………………………… 44
 加賀口門 ………………………………………… 16,44

[ま行]

松江城 ……………………………………………… 36,36
松前城 ……………………………………………… 23
松本城 ……………………………………………… 16,25,37,16,25
 天守 ……………………………………………… 16,37
松山城 ……………………………………………… 37
丸岡城天守 ………………………………………… 36,40,42,51,36,40,42,51
 天守台石垣 ……………………………………… 25,36,25

［索引　人名］

※数値の黒文字は本文の項目番号
※数値の赤文字は図版のある項目番号

明智光秀	34
朝倉氏	14,15,15
浅野氏	32,33
池田輝政	09
宇喜多	34
大谷信一	18,33
大友	34
織田信長	14,32,34,34
加藤清正	22,22
黒田官兵衛	32,34
河野	34
榊原家	33
島津	34
千姫	05
長宗我部	34
徳川家康	13,17,34,37,51,34
徳川秀忠	05
中根家	01
羽柴秀吉・秀吉	21,32,34,32,34
橋本政次	06
藤岡通夫	41
細川氏	22,22
本多家	01
本多忠政	05
本多忠刻	05
前田家	34
前田利長・光高・綱紀	34
松平忠輝	34,34
毛利	34,34
結城秀康	34
竜造寺	34

■Author
HIRAI-Kiyosi
Graduated from Tokyo Institute of Technology.
Has served as professor, Tokyo Institute of Technology : principal, Technical High School, TIT : professor, Showa Women's University : and president, Showa Women's University : director, Fukui Prefectural Museum of Cultural History.
At present, professor emeritus, Tokyo Institute of Technology, and president emeritus, Showa Women's University. D. Eng.
His field is the history of Japanese feudal residences. Recipient, NHK Broadcasting Culture Award, AIJ Prizees, Grand Prize of the Architectural Institute of Japan. He has been in charge of architectural background research for the taiga historical drama series on NHK for the past 52 years.
His books include Kenchikushi (Architectural History) (co-author); and Taiyaku Nihonjin no sumai (Bilingual: The Japanese House Then and Now) both published by Ichigaya Publishing Company.

■Translator
Hiroshi Watanabe
Graduated from Princeton University. M. Arch., Yale University. Worked at Maki and Associates.
Writer and translator.
He has translated into English many Japanese essays and books on architecture.

■Assistant
Nobuko Asano
Completed graduate school, Showa Women's University; Ph.D. Her field is the history of Japanese feudal residences.

■著　者
　平井　聖　HIRAI-Kiyosi
東京工業大学卒業。東京工業大学教授，同工学部附属工業高校校長，昭和女子大学教授，同学長，福井県立歴史博物館長。東京工業大学名誉教授　昭和女子大学名誉学長。工学博士。
専門は日本近世住宅史。放送文化賞（NHK），日本建築学会賞，同大賞を受賞。「NHK大河ドラマ」の建築考証を52年前から担当。
（市ケ谷出版社での著書）「建築史」(共著)，「対訳　日本人のすまい」

■英訳者
　渡辺　洋
アメリカ・プリンストン大学卒業。イエール大学芸術建築学部大学院修了。
槇総合計画事務所を経て，現在　建築評論家，翻訳家。
日本の建築翻訳の第一人者である。翻訳書多数。

■共同執筆
　浅野伸子
昭和女子大学大学院修了，博士(学術)。
専門は日本近世住宅史。

Bilingual **The Castles and Castle Towns of Japan**
対訳　日本の城と城下町

2017年7月10日	初版印刷
2017年7月24日	初版発行

執筆者　平　井　　聖
発行者　澤　崎　明　治
印　刷　新日本印刷　シリーズとしての表紙の基本デザイン
製　本　ブロケード　加藤三喜

発行所　株式会社　市ケ谷出版社
　　　　東京都千代田区五番町5（〒102-0076）
　　　　電話　03-3265-3711（代）
　　　　FAX　03-3265-4008
　　　　ホームページ　http://www.ichigayashuppan.co.jp

Ⓒ 2017　HIRAI-Kiyosi　　　　　　　　ISBN978-4-87071-293-5